Naturalists' Handbooks 6

Bumblebees

OLIVER E. PRŶS-JONES
Bodhaulog, St Asaph, Clwyd, North Wales

SARAH A. CORBET
Department of Zoology and Newnham College,
University of Cambridge

With illustrations by
Anthony J. Hopkins

Published for the Company of Biologists Ltd by

The Richmond Publishing Co. Ltd

P.O. Box 963, Slough, SL2 3RS, England

Series editors
S. A. Corbet and R. H. L. Disney

Published by The Richmond Publishing Co. l
P.O. Box 963, Slough, SL2 3RS
Telephone: 01753 643104
email: rpc@richmond.co.uk

First published by Cambridge University Pre
1987
This revised edition:
Text © The Company of Biologists Ltd 1991
Key illustrations © David Alford 1991
Other illustrations © Anthony J. Hopkins

Reprinted 2003

ISBN 0 85546 257 4 Paper

Printed in Great Britain

Contents

Editors' preface
Acknowledgements
1 Introduction   1
2 Distribution and recognition   2
3 The natural history of true bumblebees (*Bombus*)   6
4 Nests and their establishment in captivity   22
5 Cuckoo bumblebees (*Psithyrus*), parasites and nest
   associates   28
6 Foraging behaviour   35
7 Identification   53
   Chart A. Is the specimen a true bumblebee (*Bombus*),
   or a cuckoo bumblebee (*Psithyrus*), or neither?   54
   Chart B. Is the bumblebee a male or a female (queen
   or worker)?   55
   Quick-Check Key   55
   Main keys   57
   I: Female true bumblebees (*Bombus*)   57
   II: Male true bumblebees (*Bombus*)   62
   III: Female cuckoo bumblebees (*Psithyrus*)   67
   IV: Male cuckoo bumblebees (*Psithyrus*)   68
8 Techniques and approaches to original work   70
   Further reading   79
   Synonymy   82
   Index   83
   Distribution maps   87
   Addendum   91

*The cover illustration is designed to be used in conjunction
with the Quick-Check Key (p. 55)*

Editors' preface to second edition

The first edition of this book was published by Cambridge University Press in 1987. Since then The Richmond Publishing Co. Ltd. has taken over the Naturalists' Handbooks. This second edition includes minor corrections and an addendum (p. 91), but the major addition is the set of distribution maps based on the Bumblebee Distribution Maps Scheme atlas which is now out of print (ITE, 1980). The maps are reprinted here by kind permission of the Institute of Terrestrial Ecology (Natural Environment Research Council) and the International Bee Research Association. We hope they will stimulate readers to submit records that will make it possible to bring the maps up to date.

Students at school or university, and others without a university training in biology, may have the opportunity and inclination to study local natural history but lack the knowledge to do so in a confident and productive way. The books in this series offer them the information and ideas needed to plan an investigation, and the practical guidance to carry it out. They draw attention to regions on the frontiers of current knowledge where amateur studies have much to offer. We hope readers will derive as much satisfaction from their biological explorations as we have done.

The keys are an important feature of the books. Even in Britain, the identification of many groups remains a barrier to ecological research because experts usually write keys for other experts, and not for general ecologists. The keys in these books are meant to be easy to use. Their usefulness depends very much on the illustrations, the preparation of which was assisted by a grant from the Natural Environment Research Council.

S.A.C.
R.H.L.D.

Acknowledgements

This book is based largely on the research of O.E.P.-J., who is indebted to Professor Sir James Beament for providing facilities in the Department of Applied Biology, University of Cambridge, and to the Natural Environment Research Council and Gonville & Caius College, Cambridge, for financial support. Our appreciation of general bumblebee biology has been much enhanced by the writings of Sladen (1912, republished 1989), Free & Butler (1959), Alford (1975) and Brian (1980). The keys are based on those by Dr D.V. Alford (1975), and we are most grateful to him for permission to re-use many of his drawings to illustrate our keys. We are grateful to the Institute of Terrestrial Ecology and the International Bee Research Association for permission to re-use maps from the *Atlas of the Bumblebees of the British Isles* (1980). We would like to thank Tony Hopkins for his meticulous and beautiful artwork, G.M. Spooner, George Else and Paul Williams for commenting on the keys, and Drs John Free, Pat Willmer and Robert Prŷs-Jones, and N.J. Collar and Judith Anderson, who very kindly read and commented on the rest of the text.

O.E.P.-J.
S.A.C.

1

1 Introduction

Bumblebees are likeable creatures, and are among the most attractive of British insects and the most amenable to study. Friendlier than honeybees, they do not sting unless severely molested. Furrier, more rotund and colourful, and often larger than honeybees, and conspicuous by their deep buzz and their habit of working in gardens, they are a familiar sight in summer in town and country.

queen: a female who becomes the main egg-laying member of a nest. She ceases to forage once sufficient workers are produced

worker: a female who forages and/or looks after the nest. She usually lays few or no eggs

female: develops from a fertilised egg

male: develops from an unfertilised egg

In spring a bumblebee colony is founded by a queen, who has overwintered. Initially she lays eggs that give rise to workers. These look after the nest, defend it and collect food for it. Usually many workers are produced before eggs are laid which develop into males and young queens, who leave the nest and mate (see section 3.2).

The appeal of bumblebees as subjects for study is partly due to their predictable behaviour. Most animals are forever compromising between multiple objectives such as feeding, seeking a mate, laying eggs, and defending a territory. In contrast many of the bumblebees we see are foraging workers, whose only task is the collection of nectar and pollen to supply themselves and their colony. Because we can follow just what these foragers are doing we can begin to ask how well they are doing it, and this quantitative approach is facilitated by the ease with which the energy and water content of a flower's nectar can be measured (see sections 6.1 and 6.2).

Bumblebees are interesting too for their social behaviour. Their colonies, rather small and lasting less than a year in temperate regions, are simpler to work with than those of honeybees and can be managed quite easily in nest-boxes.

Perhaps the most important practical element of interest is the role of bumblebees as pollinators, often underestimated and still poorly understood. Much more needs to be known about them as pollinators of crops and about their nesting requirements and biology – particularly now, when the countryside is changing, the number of bumblebee species is declining locally, and some valuable bee-pollinated crops are suffering unpredictable variations in yield.

2 Distribution and recognition

2.1 Distribution

The world fauna of bumblebees, about 300 species, is centred on the north temperate zone, extending through Europe, Asia and North America. Apart from a few species in South America, the only bumblebees in the southern hemisphere are some in the East Indian archipelago, and British species that were established in New Zealand in the nineteenth century. Recently, a British species, *Bombus ruderatus*, appears to have become established in South America, having been introduced from New Zealand. Arguments in favour of introducing a species to a new area should be very carefully balanced against the possible adverse effects of the introduction on the native flora and fauna.

The British bumblebee fauna of 25 species (19 *Bombus*, 6 *Psithyrus*) contains representatives of a wide range of subgeneric groups, and we are fortunate in having a correspondingly wide diversity of ecology and behaviour to study.

When we compare the present distribution of true bumblebees, *Bombus* species, in mainland Britain with records made before 1960, it is apparent that there have been marked changes in recent decades (Williams, 1982).[*] Six species are widespread and fairly abundant over much of Britain, and you can probably see most of them in any year: *B. pascuorum* Scopoli, *B. lucorum* (L.), *B. hortorum* (L.), *B. pratorum* (L.), *B. terrestris* (L.) and *B. lapidarius* (L.). Five species are very local and restricted to southern Britain, and their distributions have contracted: *B. ruderatus* (Fabr.), *B. sylvarum* (L.), *B. humilis* Illiger, *B. subterraneus* (L.) and *B. ruderarius* (Müller). Four others are widespread but very patchy, and have disappeared from many localities: *B. muscorum* (L.), *B. monticola* Smith, *B. soroeensis* (Fabr.) and *B. jonellus* (Kirby). *B. magnus* Kruger is considered here as a species, distinct from *B. lucorum*, but its true status is far from clear; it is associated with moorland areas in the north and west. *B. distinguendus* Morawitz is now rare and mainly restricted to coastal sites, while the other two species, *B. cullumanus* (Kirby) and *B. pomorum* (Panzer), have not been recorded for many years.

---

[*] References cited under the authors' names in the text appear in full in Further Reading on p. 79.

The map (fig. 1) shows where the three main biogeographic elements occur in Britain, and will give you some idea of how many bumblebee species to expect around your home. Over much of the country there are only six species. Although this impoverishment of the fauna makes identification easier, it must be regarded as a conservation problem. In Britain no records are available to tell us whether or not the decline in bumblebee species distributions has been accompanied by a decrease in local abundance, or whether these changes have had a significant impact on crop pollination. However in New Zealand recent work (Macfarlane, Griffin & Read, 1983) has

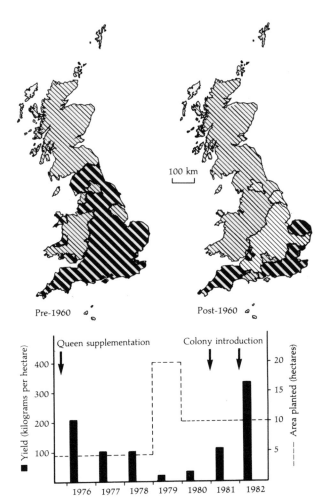

Fig. 1. Pre-1960 and post-1960 distributions of *Bombus* species in England, Wales and Scotland. **Widespread throughout** (broad and narrow lines): *B. pascuorum, B. lucorum, B. terrestris, B. pratorum, B. hortorum* and *B. lapidarius*. **Local and southern** (broad lines): *B. ruderarius, B. sylvarum , B. humilis, B. subterraneus* and *B. ruderatus*. **Local but widespread** (dots): *B. muscorum, B. monticola, B. soroeensis* and *B. jonellus*. Even in the areas where they occur, these last two groups of bees are not usually common. From Williams (1982), by permission of the International Bee Research Association.

Pre-1960   Post-1960   100 km

Fig. 2. Effect of releasing queen bumblebees in spring, and introducing *B. hortorum* colonies in nest-boxes at flowering, on yields of Red Clover seed in New Zealand. After Macfarlane & others (1983).

Queen supplementation   Colony introduction

Yield (kilograms per hectare)

Area planted (hectares)

1976 1977 1978 1979 1980 1981 1982

Year

shown that supplementing bumblebee populations can
dramatically increase seed yields (fig. 2).

The distributions of bumblebees in Ireland are still
poorly known and deserve much more study (see
pp. 87–90)

2.2 Recognising bumblebees

There should be no difficulty in recognising a bumblebee
by sight and by sound. Plates 1–4 show you what they
look like. True bumblebees are all members of the genus
Bombus (meaning 'booming'). Cuckoo bumblebees,
members of the genus *Psithyrus* (meaning 'murmuring'),
resemble true bumblebees but have a softer buzz, a
sparser coat of hair showing the shiny black cuticle
through it, and no pollen-collecting apparatus on their
legs. Cuckoo bumblebees are inquilines in the nests of
true bumblebees (see section 5.1).

inquiline: an animal living in
the home of another species,
and using its food

With a little experience it soon becomes possible to
recognise most of the common species of *Bombus* and
Psithyrus in the field, without disturbing them, on the
basis of colour pattern. This is a valuable asset in ecological studies. The Quick-Check Key (p. 55) and the colour
plates should help to make this possible. Initially,
though, it will be necessary to catch and anaesthetise or
kill a few bees of each type in order to name them.

There are several distinct colour patterns among British
bumblebees. Surprisingly, each is adopted not by one
species only, but by a group of species that may not be
closely related to each other at all (e.g. *B. lapidarius,
B. ruderarius, B. pomorum, B. cullumanus* and *P. rupestris*
Lepeletier). These are apparently examples of Müllerian
mimicry. A predator that gets stung whenever it tries to
eat a bee with a particular colour pattern will eventually
learn to associate the colour pattern with a painful sting
and therefore to avoid it. The commoner the colour
pattern that a bee wears, the sooner predators will learn
to avoid it. A bee can therefore reduce the risk of getting
eaten by sharing a common uniform with many other
bees of the same or different species. These Müllerian
mimicry groups involve cuckoo bumblebees as well as
true bumblebees, and can confuse ecologists as well as
.predators.

2.3 Reading about bumblebees

The first major book on British bumblebees was F.W.L.
Sladen's *The Humble-bee, its Life History and how to
Domesticate it*, first published in 1912. With superb coloured
illustrations and delightful anecdotal accounts of the species,

reflecting acute biological observation, this excellent book has recently been republished (Sladen, 1989). Free & Butler's *Bumblebees*, published in 1959 but now out of print, was a worthy successor, and included a field key by Yarrow which, for the first time, made it possible for beginners to name their bees. Alford's *Bumblebees* (1975) covers the biology of bumblebees and their associates and parasites, and includes a key, more critical but harder to use than Free & Butler's. That key was the basis for the Bumblebee Distribution Maps Scheme that gave so much valuable information on bumblebee distribtuion before it ended in 1976. A brief popular account of bumblebee biology appears in Alford's *The Life of the Bumblebee* (1978).

North American bumblebees are considered in Plath's *Bumblebees and their Ways* (1943), which has long been out of print, while Heinrich's *Bumblebee Economics* (1979), also based on work in North America, describes some fascinating aspects of bumblebee ecology and physiology.

British bumblebees' names have changed from time to time, and some of the names in use now are different from those in earlier books. In this book we use the names given in the checklist by Fitton and others (1978), but we retain *B. magnus* (Alford, 1975). Names and synonyms are listed on p. 82.

3 The natural history of true bumblebees (*Bombus*)

3.1 Natural history

The different species of true bumblebee are alike in some aspects of their biology, for example in the main features of their life cycle (section 3.2), but very different in others. Some of the idiosyncrasies of British species begin to emerge from intensive studies of their ecology (see table 1). To illustrate this point we shall introduce four of the commonest species.

Bombus terrestris (of the earth; from the Latin *terra*)
In spring the gigantic queens of *B. terrestris* are among the first to emerge from hibernation (fig. 3). Occasionally, if cold weather is followed by a warm spell, some queens emerge in midwinter, and will even attempt to nest if flowers are available (Prŷs-Jones, 1982).

In most species the queen and worker have the same coloured tail, but British *B. terrestris* queens have brownish tails and workers usually have white or buff ones (pl. 1.3 and 1.4). Towards the end of the nesting period some workers have queen-like coloration. The reason for this is not clear, but it may be that declining vigour of the queen eventually allows the expression of at least some queen-like characteristics in all the female offspring (see p. 15, 'complex' species).

Most workers of *B. terrestris* look quite similar to those of *B. lucorum*, and small individuals can be difficult to separate. Both species have a short broad face and a relatively short tongue, features associated with their habit of collecting nectar from rather short open flowers. They also have the ability to bite a hole in the corolla tube

corolla: tube or crown of petals

Fig. 3. Maximum soil temperature (at a depth of 30 centimetres) on the day spring queens were first observed. Letters indicate species: *B. pratorum* (P), *B. terrestris* (T), *B. lucorum* (L), *B. ruderarius* (R), *B. pascuorum* (A), *B. lapidarius* (D) and *B. hortorum* (H). Values are mean ± standard error; for an introduction to statistics see Parker (1979). From Prŷs-Jones (1982).

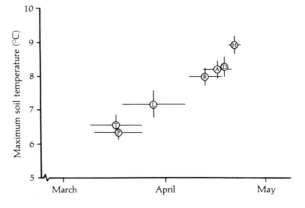

of longer flowers (fig. 4), such as Honeysuckle *Lonicera periclymenum* L., Comfrey *Symphytum officinale* L. and Field Bean *Vicia faba* L. This enables them to extract nectar which they would be unable to reach from the front of the flower. In Britain only queens and workers of *B. terrestris* and *B. lucorum* have been observed to rob flowers regularly in this way, but other bumblebees (even honeybees) often re-use the holes, acting as secondary robbers.

Table 1. *Life history information for six common British bumblebees*

	B. lapidarius	*B. lucorum*	*B. terrestris*	*B. pratorum*	*B. pascuorum*	*B. hortorum*
% visits for:						
Nectar-only	75	71	80	23	60	38
Nectar + pollen	13	1	9	67	33	57
Pollen-only	12	28	11	10	7	5
No. of observations	*216*	*85*	*192*	*184*	*258*	*159*
Pollen-only visits as a % of all pollen visits	48	96	56	13	17	8
% visits according to orientation of flower entrance:						
Down	0	1	7	39	13	16
Horizontal	35	38	40	28	61	71
Up	65	61	53	33	26	13
% visits to separate (as opposed to clustered) flowers	46	61	62	81	82	93
No. of observations	*210*	*84*	*188*	*177*	*254*	*159*
Average corolla depth visited (mm) (nectar-only and nectar + pollen visits)	5.1	5.1	6.3	7.4	8.3	8.7
No. of observations	*139*	*59*	*168*	*100*	*351*	*133*
Average tongue length (mm)	8.1	7.2	8.2	7.1	8.6	13.5
Pocket-maker (M) or pollen-storer (S)	S	S	S	S	M	M
Predominant nest-site (U, underground; S, surface)	U	U	U	S	S	S
Colony size	Large	Large	Large	Small	Small–medium	Small–medium
First workers observed	May–June	May	May	Apr.–May	May–June	May
Max. nos. of workers observed:	Aug.	Aug.	July–Aug.	June	Aug.	June–July
Length of life cycle	Medium	Long	Long	Short	Long	Short
Evidence for 2nd cycle of colony activity	No	No	No	Yes	No	Yes
Relative degree of size variation (foraging workers)	Little	Little	Little	Moderate	Large	Large
Worker/queen size overlap	None	None	None	Slight	Moderate	Moderate

Summarised from Prŷs-Jones (1982). Based on regular observations throughout the life cycle of each species. Numerical data apply to foraging workers.

Fig. 4. *B. terrestris* worker taking nectar 'illegally', through a hole she has bitten in a honeysuckle flower.

Sometimes almost every flower in a Field Bean crop may be robbed. It is hard to evaluate the impact this has on crop pollination. On the one hand one might expect that bees removing nectar in this way, without contacting the anthers and stigma, would impair pollination. On the other hand it has been suggested that robbery may sometimes cause long-tongued bumblebees, that do not rob, to visit more flowers for each load of nectar, so enhancing pollen transfer. Hole-biting may attract more honeybees to a clover crop, but if most of these are gathering nectar via rob-holes they may fail to effect cross-pollination. Probably the most important consideration is that pollen-collecting bees are unaffected by hole-biting and remain successful pollinators – which may account for the fact that robbery of Red Clover does not appear to decrease seed set (Hawkins, 1961). Certainly in New Zealand, where introduced bumblebees are very important pollinators of Red Clover, robbery by *B. terrestris* is common, yet in areas where this species is the main visitor to the crop it is still a useful pollinator (Gurr, 1975).

In situations where there is a wide choice of flower types *B. terrestris* rarely uses pendulous flowers, probably because it is not very agile. Instead it usually selects flowers that face upwards or horizontally and provide a substantial landing platform (table 1).

As its name implies, this bumblebee often nests in the ground, commonly adopting the disused nest of a small mammal (see section 4.1). It starts nesting early in the season and has a long cycle, reaching peak numbers in July (fig. 5), when colonies may contain several hundred workers. Sladen (1912) was among the first to note that workers of *B. terrestris* are more defensive than those of other species, so although its nests are among the easiest to find, they are not the easiest to work with.

B. hortorum (of the garden; from the Latin *hortus*)
A white-tailed bumblebee with yellow bands (pl. 1.5), *B. hortorum* differs from *B. terrestris* most obviously in a detail of pattern – it has a yellow band at the rear of the thorax – and in its long narrow face and long tongue, longer than that of any other common British species (fig. 6). With a long tongue comes the ability to take nectar from flowers with long tubular corollas, and *B. hortorum* specialises on these. It is among the best pollinators of Field Bean (Free, 1970) and Red Clover (Holm, 1966; Gurr, 1975).

Most often it visits relatively nectar-rich flowers such as Honeysuckle, *Delphinium* species, and Balsam *Impatiens glandulifera* Royle that have openings facing horizontally, and are arranged singly, so that a bee must fly from one flower to the next (fig. 7). In this respect *B. hortorum* contrasts markedly with, for example, *B. lapidarius* (pl. 2.1 and 2.2) which shows a strong tendency to visit massed flowers such as members of the family Compositae (Knapweed *Centaurea nigra* L. is a favourite); these are often nectar-poor, but a bee can probe many flowers (or florets) between flights. Differences between species in

Fig. 5. Seasonal cycles of flight activity of four common *Bombus* species at Cambridge in 1978. From Prŷs-Jones (1982).

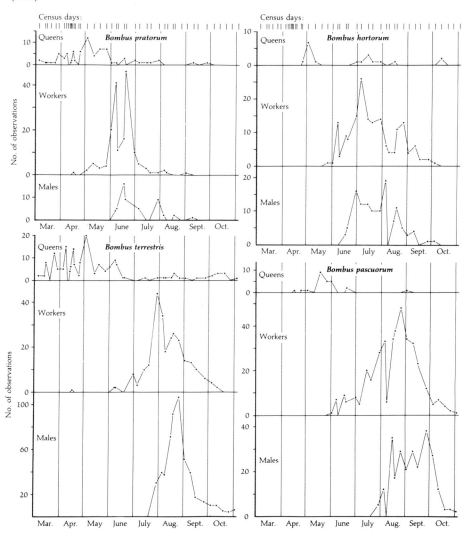

Fig. 6. Species differences in
tongue length.

B. hortorum ♀

B. pascuorum ♀

B. pratorum ♀

Fig. 7. *B. hortorum* visiting
Nasturtium *Tropaeolum majus*
L.

enzyme activity of the flight musculature may partly
account for such differences in foraging behaviour (see
section 6.1).

Although *B. hortorum* is Britain's most widespread
bumblebee species, individuals are seldom very abundant, possibly because the long-tubed flowers that they
visit are relatively uncommon. Queens are late to emerge
(fig. 3) and start nest-building in spring; colonies are quite
small, often producing no more than about 30–80 workers. Males and young queens are sometimes reared from
only the second or third mass of eggs to be laid, and will
have been produced in most nests by the middle of July
(fig. 5).

Related to the short life cycle of the colony are indications that this species possesses the unusual ability to
complete a second nesting cycle in some years (Prŷs-
Jones, 1982; see fig. 11), whilst most bumblebee species
can complete only one. The other short cycle species,
B. jonellus (pl. 1.6 and 1.7) and *B. pratorum* (p. 11; pl. 2.5
and 2.6), almost certainly do so too on occasion. As yet
the evidence is very suggestive, but not conclusive. More
is needed (see pp. 20 and 21).

Nests of *B. hortorum* are hard to find because there are
so few workers going in and coming out to draw attention
to them. Nests are usually placed among plant roots and
litter just above or just below the soil surface.

B. pascuorum (of the pastures; from the Latin *pascuum*)

B. pascuorum is distinctive as the only common species to
have a uniformly ginger-coloured thorax. The abdomen,
too, is gingery, but there is much variation in the colour
(ranging from foxy-red to almost grey) and in the intensity
of the darker markings (pl. 3.5–3.7). This is another
long-tongued bumblebee (fig. 6). It resembles *B. hortorum*
in taking nectar from long, tubular flowers, but *B. pascuorum* is more catholic in its flower choice. As in *B. hortorum* the workers tend to visit flowers that face sideways
(table 1) – White Dead-nettle *Lamium album* L. is a favourite. Unlike *B. hortorum*, this bumblebee shows a sex-
related difference in foraging habits: males visit clustered
or compound flowers, such as Marsh Thistle *Cirsium
palustre* (L.) Scop., much more often than workers do.

B. pascuorum is one of five British species known as
'carder bees' (subgenus *Thoracobombus*) because of their
distinctive habit of carding (combing) together material
from around the nest to form a covering for the cells
(Sladen, 1912). Nests are built among vegetation on or
just below the soil surface. The bees gather together the
covering material with their mandibles and legs, often
standing facing outwards from the colony, passing the

moss or grass stems backwards between their legs in a
scrabbling fashion.

Colonies vary in size, but can be relatively large, containing up to about 200 workers. They are also long-lived,
often lasting into October, being slow to develop to their
full strength (fig. 5). A patch of Water Figwort *Scrophularia
auriculata* L. or Marsh Woundwort *Stachys palustris* L.
close to a nest may be alive with foragers of *B. pascuorum*,
and they are potentially valuable pollinators of deep-
flowered crops. Unfortunately, along with other surface-
nesters, the species suffers badly when areas of rough
grass are mown. Ploughing also removes hibernation
sites, as well as underground nesting places used by
other species. This serves to emphasise the importance of
leaving some suitable areas undisturbed.

B. pratorum (of the meadows; from the Latin *pratum*)
A small black bumblebee with yellow bands and an
orange tail, *B. pratorum* is one of the simplest species to
recognise in the field (pl. 2.5 and 2.6). Its tongue is of only
moderate length (fig. 6), but its flower selection includes
a wider range of corolla depth than this would suggest.
At one extreme it will visit very short, open flowers; at the
other, it makes use of some long tubular flowers by
thrusting the whole of its relatively narrow head into the
corolla. A very agile bumblebee, it commonly visits
flowers that hang downwards, and is often seen acrobati-
cally hanging upside down to work a flower of Comfrey
or Snowberry *Symphoricarpos rivularis* Suksdorf.

B. pratorum is good at working in low temperatures and
it can be seen early in the morning, adopting a characteristic flight pattern in which hovering alternates with dart-
ing flight. The species appears early in the spring, and
colonies are established in April and May. At maturity, in
late June and July, nests may contain only a handful of
workers or they may occasionally be large, with up to
about 200 workers. Compared with other species, workers begin to be seen foraging relatively soon after queens
emerge from hibernation, and worker numbers peak well
in advance of other species. The cycle is short, and the
first generation ends in midsummer (fig. 5). Most of the
young queens then begin their period of overwintering,
at soil temperatures well above those at which they will
emerge the following spring. However, as in *B. hortorum*,
which also has a short cycle, a few young *B. pratorum*
queens appear to go on to produce a second cycle in some
years.

The nests of *B. pratorum* are constructed in a wide
variety of sites above, on and below ground. It is not
uncommon for disused birds' nests to be occupied,
particularly those in nest-boxes (see section 4.1).

3.2 The annual cycle

A honeybee colony is potentially immortal, and its queen does no foraging. Honeybees overwinter as a cluster of workers with their queen and a store of honey. On the first warm days of spring these workers emerge from the hive to forage for nectar and pollen with which to feed themselves and to support the development of new workers, building up the colony towards summer. The colony can persist through the winter because of the honey store. Workers are therefore present in spring so the queen herself need not forage, but can stay at home laying eggs.

Fig. 8. Outline life cycle of *Bombus* in a temperate region, such as Britain (variations that are sometimes found in the arctic, the tropics and at high altitude are mentioned on pp. 20 and 21).

Bumblebees do things differently (fig. 8). In temperate regions colonies die out in autumn, and only the young

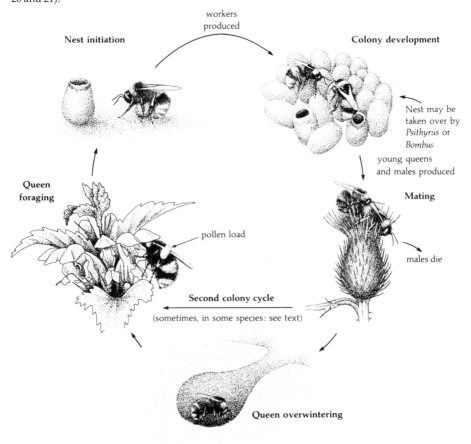

Nest initiation

workers
produced

Colony development

Nest may be taken over by *Psithyrus* or *Bombus*

young queens and males produced

Queen foraging

Mating

pollen load

males die

Second colony cycle

(sometimes, in some species: see text)

Queen overwintering

mated queens overwinter. Alone, therefore, they establish new colonies in spring.

In late summer a young queen may be seen exploring the ground. When she finds a suitable site – often a north-facing bank which will not be warmed by the winter sun – she burrows several centimetres into the soil. Here she overwinters. Dissection of a queen caught seeking a hibernation site reveals a massive clear or white fat body, that may occupy most of the abdominal cavity. Most of this will be used up as a food reserve during winter; in spring the fat body is almost exhausted.

fat body: a mass of food storage cells, mainly in the abdomen, containing fat, glycogen and protein

When the soil temperature rises in spring the queen emerges from hibernation (fig. 3), and may be seen sunning herself or foraging on early flowers such as Pussy Willow *Salix* species, White Dead-nettle or Flowering Currant *Ribes sanguineum* Pursh. Her behaviour will change in a predictable way as colony foundation proceeds (fig. 9). At first she forages only for herself, eating large quantities of pollen and nectar while her ovaries develop, and roosting at night under moss and other vegetation. She then seeks a place to establish her nest. Nest-searching queens fly to and fro, low over banks and rough uncultivated land, sometimes investigating dark holes, crawling briefly into cavities and tussocks. The search often ends in the disused nest of a small mammal or bird. It appears that *Bombus* queens quite often search out and fight for established nests – which represent a

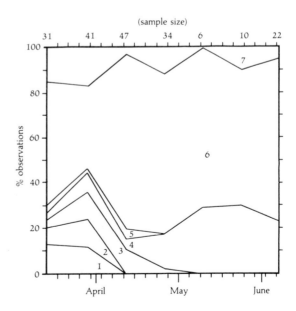

Fig. 9. Behaviour of *B. terrestris* queens after emergence from overwintering sites. 1, inactive; 2, sunning; 3, eating pollen; 4, nest-searching; 5, collecting pollen; 6, collecting nectar; 7, flying. From Prŷs-Jones (1982).

valuable resource in terms of time and energy – particularly if nest-sites are scarce or the season is short. It is not
unusual to find several dead queens, of the same or
different species, in the entrance of the newly established
nest (see p. 23).

Having found a suitable site, the queen adjusts the
nesting material to form a small chamber. She then goes
out to collect pollen, which she brings back to the nest,
packed in the pollen baskets on her hind legs. The pollen
is moulded into a mass that forms the base of the egg
clump. In an untidy cell made of wax (extruded from
between the plates of her abdomen) and pollen, built on
the pollen mass, the queen lays her first batch of eggs.
Within convenient reach of the egg clump she constructs
a thimble-like wax honeypot. This she stocks with nectar.
Taking occasional sips of nectar, she broods the egg
clump, warming it by contact with the lower, less hairy
surface of her abdomen. Bumblebees have considerable
control over her body temperature (see p. 36; a brooding queen can keep her body at about 30 °C, and maintain
her egg clump at 30–32 °C, despite low outside temperatures (Heinrich, 1979). During this stage of colony
development the queen spends much of her time in the
nest, brooding the eggs, and makes only occasional
foraging trips.

Eggs hatch after 4–6 days. The resulting larvae feed on
the pollen mass, and are supplied by the queen with
nectar and pollen, in a manner that depends on the
species (see below). At first, the larvae remain together in
their cell, which the queen enlarges to accommodate their
growth as they progress through a series of larval moults.
Later, each spins a delicate silken cocoon, creating a
chamber of its own. After 10–20 days as a larva, a much
tougher, neater, cylindrical cocoon is formed, in which
the larva discharges faecal material (meconium) which
has accumulated in its gut throughout life. It then pupates
(fig. 10).

Fig. 10. *Bombus* pupa in an opened cocoon.

At this stage the queen scrapes the pollen/wax mixture
from the pupal cocoons. She re-uses it to construct one or
more chambers, between or on top of the cocoons, in
which she lays her second batch of eggs. In some species
(e.g. *B. hortorum, B. pratorum*) these egg clumps, like the
first, are primed with a pollen mass; in others they are not
(Free & Butler, 1959).

Adult workers emerge after about 2 weeks as pupae.
Each bites her way out of her cocoon, often helped by the
queen or other workers. At first pale silvery-grey, tousled
and soft-winged, the worker acquires her full colours and
fluffy appearance after a few hours, and her wings harden
within about a day. New workers soon begin foraging, as

well as helping the queen to tend the brood. Once there are enough of them to take over foraging duties the queen remains within the nest, where she devotes herself to housework and egg-laying.

Species differ in the way they feed pollen to the larvae. 'Pocket-makers' construct waxen pouches or pockets near the base of the larval chamber or brood clump. Into these, the returning foragers deposit their loads of pollen; the larvae feed from the resulting mass. Later, the queen (or workers) may supplement this diet by regurgitating a nectar/pollen mixture into the brood chamber, through a temporary hole in the wax envelope. The larvae of a batch remain together, sharing a common chamber and the pollen supply that goes with it.

In the other group of species, the 'pollen-storers', pollen brought into the nest is not put into pockets in the brood clump, but instead is stored in empty pupal cocoons and specially constructed wax cells or cylinders. The queen or workers then feed it to the larvae, bit by bit, squirting a regurgitated mixture of nectar and pollen into the larval cell through a hole in the wax covering.

Instead of continuing to share a common chamber as they mature, the larvae of pollen-storing species spin separate compartments, and they are fed individually. This has two consequences. First, it is much harder to 'read' the history of a colony from the arrangement of the chambers in pollen-storers than it is in pocket-makers. Secondly, it appears to influence pathways of development. Workers from a single colony may vary widely in size, probably because of differences in the amounts of food each received as a larva. Larvae of pollen-storers, fed individually, receive fair shares of food. In contrast, larvae of a pocket-maker do better or worse according to both the degree of larval competition and position in relation to the pocket (Sladen, 1912; Cumber, 1949). Thus size variability is said to be less marked in pollen-storers (e.g. *B. terrestris, B. pratorum*) than in pocket-makers (e.g. *B. hortorum, B. pascuorum*). Table 1 shows which species belong to each group.

When the colony is mature some eggs develop not into workers, but into males and queens. Just what influences the changeover to sexual production is not well understood. Adequate food stores, a particular worker/larva ratio, chemical cues, nest temperature stability and bee density in the nest, are probably all influential factors. Their relative importance appears to vary with the species concerned. At least two groups of species can be distinguished: 'simple' and 'complex' (Brian, 1980). In simple bumblebees there is no obvious influence of the queen over brood rearing. Whether a female larva becomes a worker or a queen does not appear to be determined until just before the larval/pupal transition; possibly it is not always fixed even then. Larvae that become queens have usually eaten for longer and grown more than those that become workers. Such species include, in Britain, *B. pratorum* and probably *B. hortorum*. In contrast, in complex bumblebees, such as *B. terrestris* and perhaps *B. lapidarius*, the queen can, probably with the aid of pheromones, stop the workers feeding the larvae with sufficient quantity and/or frequency for them to develop into queens, even at high worker/larva ratios when ample food is available.

pheromone: a substance produced by an animal that influences the behaviour or physiological development of another individual of the same species

Thus complex species can delay queen production, allowing the build-up of large worker populations. One can speculate that in general species with large colonies and long life cycles (i.e. many pollen-storers) may well be complex species, while those with small, short-cycle colonies (i.e. many pocket-makers) are probably simple species.

As a result of the differing methods of queen production in the two groups, queens are usually distinctly larger than workers in complex species (having fed better for a longer period), but in simple species they cannot be distinguished on size alone (having merely fed a little longer at the end of their larval life). The real differences between a queen and a worker (Definitions, p. 1) are physiological and behavioural. A queen can mate and develop her ovaries, and is the colony member who is primarily active in egg-laying. Unlike a worker, a queen *may* also hibernate and build up in autumn the abundant reserves in her fat body that will keep her alive through the winter. To be sure whether an individual is a queen or a worker, it is necessary to know how she functions in the colony; an indication of this may be gained by dissecting

spermatheca: the sac in which sperm are stored after mating

her. The presence of sperm in her spermatheca indicates that she has mated successfully (technique, p. 72). It is probably uncommon for workers to mate, and therefore a fertilised bumblebee with mature eggs in her ovary is almost certainly a queen. Further, in autumn, a female bumblebee with an abundant fat body must be a young queen.

In bees, unfertilised eggs give rise to males and fertilised eggs produce females (queens and workers). An unmated bee can lay only male eggs, but a mated female can determine the sex of her egg by controlling the release of sperm from her spermatheca. A few males are produced early in the season, perhaps from eggs laid by workers or unfertilised queens. The proportion of males (and, if fertilised workers are present, the proportion of females) derived from worker-laid eggs remains to be determined. Probably it varies with the species and the conditions.

Although some colonies produce only male or female sexual forms, or neither, most produce both, the males somewhat in advance of the young queens. Males play no part in looking after the colony except for a little incidental brooding; they leave the nest and seldom or never return. Their sole function is to mate with young queens. They forage rather slowly, for themselves alone, sleeping out at night, often clinging under the heads of flowers such as thistles and knapweeds. Young queens go out foraging, but they do not normally help to provision the colony; unlike males, they often return to the nest at night. Those who collect pollen appear to do so only when their mother has died, or lost her dominant status. Such young queens usually contain developed eggs (Prŷs-Jones, 1982) and are probably laying in their parental nest.

The reproductive behaviour of male bumblebees is conspicuous and unusual. Individual males patrol characteristic routes, circuiting the same flight path, pausing on the wing at intervals at certain features such as a particular leaf, stone or area of tree trunk. These features, visited repeatedly through the day, sometimes carry a species-specific scent detectable by the human nose (Sladen, 1912). They are places where, early in the morning, the male bumblebee has deposited a scent-mark, a fragrant mixture of compounds secreted by a gland – once thought to be the mandibular gland, but now known to be primarily the labial gland (Kullenberg and others, 1973) – that opens between the mandibles. Many of these compounds have been identified and found to be fatty acid derivatives and terpene alcohols and esters (table 2).

How can a queen find a male of her own species? The species differ from one another in the mixture of compounds that make up their characteristic scents and in the nature of the route the males patrol – along a low hedgerow or at treetop level for instance. It is assumed that queens visit the scent-marked trail, and that mating takes place here, but bumblebees have rarely been seen mating in the wild. Work done in Scandinavia (Bringer, 1973; Svensson, 1979) shows the flight levels of some *Bombus* and *Psithyrus* species that are also found in Britain (table 3). Are similar patterns found here? It would be interesting to know to what extent flight levels are charac-teristic of a species, and to what extent they vary with the habitat.

Even after mating, a young queen may continue to return for a while to the nest where she grew up. By eating large quantities of nectar and pollen she builds up her fat body, and as an additional food store she fills her highly distensible honeystomach with thick honey. She then seeks a site in which to overwinter.

Queens and males are the colony's contribution to the next generation. They are the last brood to be reared;

Table 2. *Composition of the male marking substances*

	Bombus	B. pratorum	B. jonellus	B. soroeensis	B. lapidarius	B. pascuorum	B. monticola	B. terrestris	B. lucorum	Psithyrus	P. rupestris	P. bohemicus	P. campestris	P. barbutellus	P. sylvestris
Geraniol	○														
Citronellol	○											◉			
Geranyl acetate	○														
Citronellyl acetate	○														
Farnesene isomers	○														
All-*trans*-farnesol	●													●	
2,3-dihydro-6-*trans*-farnesol		●						●							
2,3-dihydro-6-*trans*-farnesal			◉												
All-*trans*-farnesyl acetate	◉													◉	
2,3-dihydrofarnesyl acetate								○							
Geranylgeraniol	○								○						
Geranylcitronellol								◉			○				
Geranylgeranyl acetate	◉		●						○		◉				
Tetradecanal											○				◉
Tetradecanol					○						○				
Hexadecenol					●	●					●	●			●
Hexadecanal															○
Hexadecenal						●						○			◉
Hexadecanol	◉			◉			◉	○	○		○				
Octadecenol	◉												◉	○	
Eicosenol											●				
Hexadecenyl acetate							●								
Hexadecyl acetate							◉		○						
Octadecyl acetate														○	
Eicosyl acetate									○						
Docosyl acetate									○						
Ethyl decanoate								○	○						
Ethyl dodecanoate								◉	●						
Ethyl tetradecenoate								○	●						
Ethyl tetradecanoate									○						
Ethyl hexadecatrienoate									○						
Ethyl hexadecadienoate									○						
Ethyl hexadecenoate									○						
Ethyl octadecatrienoate									○						
Ethyl octadecadienoate									○						
Ethyl octadecenoate									○						
Ethyl octadecanoate									○						
Tetradecenoic acid															◉

Symbols indicate relative amount present: minor component (○), major component (◉) and main component (●).

Adapted from Bergström & others (1981), Cederberg & others (1984) and Descoins & others (1984).

when they have left, the old nest has no further role to play. The few remaining workers forage only for themselves and behave more like males when visiting flowers, moving slowly and lethargically. Like the males, they will have died off by the end of the season.

Seasonal timing of events in the colony cycle varies with the species, with the geographical area, and with weather conditions in a particular year (Prŷs-Jones, 1982). We have seen that the large queens of *B. terrestris* are among the first to emerge from hibernation in spring, but their colonies are not among the quickest to develop. It is often little *B. pratorum* whose workers appear first. *B. pratorum*, a short-cycle species, is also one of the earliest to produce males and new queens: these frequently appear early in the summer in May or June, occasionally before some of the other species have produced their first workers. By about August the latest species have begun to produce males and queens, and by October even the slow-maturing nests of *B. pascuorum* are over or on the decline (fig. 5).

Overwintered spring queens found in colonies cannot be confused with new virgin queens, produced late in the summer, because they appear at different seasons and they look and behave differently. An overwintered spring queen has often worn away the fine hairs (micro-

Table 3. *Flight levels of various* Bombus *and* Psithyrus *species in coniferous forest in Sweden*

Flight level (metres above ground)	B. lapidarius	B. lucorum	B. pascuorum	B. terrestris	B. sylvarum	B. pratorum	B. hortorum	P. bohemicus	P. campestris	P. rupestris	P. sylvestris
16–17	O										
	O										
14–15	O										
	O										
12–13	O										
	O										
10–11	O										
	O										
8–9	O							O			
	O							O			
6–7	O							O			
	O	O						O			
4–5		O	O					O	O	O	
		O	O	O	O			O	O		
2–3		O	O	O	O	O		O	O	O	
	O	O	O	O	O	O		O	O	O	
0–1	O	O	O	O		O	O	O	O	O	O

Adapted from Bringer (1973).

trichia) on her wings, and her wingtips rapidly become ragged as she forages in a business-like way for nectar and pollen for her brood. Her fat body is by now almost exhausted and looks yellowish, but her ovaries contain mature or ripening eggs. A newly emerged queen in late summer is, by contrast, fresh and unworn. Her fat body appears white or clear and is building up for hibernation, and her ovaries are undeveloped (she will not lay eggs until the next year). Generally she forages only for herself and therefore does not carry pollen (see p. 17).

We have mentioned that a few species (*B. hortorum*, *B. pratorum* and *B. jonellus*) may sometimes produce a second colony life cycle within one season. This means that some of the new queens that emerge from the nest and mate in summer do not hibernate, but instead at once establish nests (or take over their parental nests) and begin worker production. If you see a fresh unworn queen collecting pollen, at a season when old spring queens are confined to their nests, she may be a young queen founding a second-generation colony. This exciting possibility can be investigated by dissection: she would have mature eggs in her ovary, sperm in her spermatheca, and sparse yellowish-brown fat (see techniques, p. 72). However, instead of killing her, it would, if possible, be most informative to follow her home and gently inspect the nest. Has she started a new nest of her own, is she nesting and laying her eggs in the remains of her mother's nest, or is she simply foraging for her parental nest? Alternatively, you can encourage a young queen to found her colony in a nest-box (fig. 11; see sections 4.3 and 4.4) and follow events that way. This procedure has the disadvantage of being conducted under unnatural conditions, but the advantage that you know for certain that you are dealing with a queen that has not overwintered, and, if successful, it at least shows that overwintering is not a necessary preliminary to nesting in that species.

As we have seen, in Britain, the bumblebee foraging season (and, because they do not store much honey, the active season) differs between species – in some cases to a considerable degree (see *B. pratorum* and *B. terrestris* in fig. 5). This may, in part, reflect competition for food. However, the extent of any temporal segregation of species is limited by a shortage of flowers in winter. Further north and at higher altitudes the season is even shorter, and it is the short-cycle species that extend furthest towards the North Pole. Nearer the Equator flowers are sometimes available throughout the year. In the South American tropics bumblebee colonies may last several years, producing enormous numbers of workers

Fig. 11. *B. hortorum*: a young queen that has not overwintered brooding her first batch of eggs.

(see Michener, 1974). In middle latitudes (about 40° N or S), such as New Zealand (Cumber, 1954; Gurr, 1973), and Corsica too (Ferton, 1901), colonies may survive through the winter.

Length of the life cycle can also vary with latitude within species (Prŷs-Jones, 1982). Some bumblebees which in Britain have long cycles (e.g. *B. terrestris*, *B. ruderatus*), appear capable of extending their life cycles at lower latitudes. Species with short cycles (e.g. *B. hortorum*, *B. pratorum*, *B. jonellus*) apparently do not do this – although they may complete a second cycle if the season is long enough. *B. pascuorum* is interesting in that it has a long cycle in Britain (50°–60° N) and yet it occurs as far north as 70° N. Presumably different populations of *B. pascuorum* (which may correspond with the many described subspecies) are adapted to different climatic conditions.

4 Nests and their establishment in captivity

4.1 Natural nests

A great variety of nest-sites chosen by queen bumblebees are structures built by other animals, that are taken over when the original owner has finished with them. Most species commonly use nests of small mammals. The more adaptable species (*B. terrestris, B. lucorum, B. pratorum* and *B. lapidarius*) take advantage of man's artefacts. *B. terrestris* will nest in surprising places. We have found nests in a rolled-up carpet and a disused armchair, under an old lawnmower and an upturned sink, in a heap of coal, and often in or under a garden shed. *B. pratorum* is probably the most versatile British species: a disused Robin's nest suspended over a pond, bird boxes, an old cushion, lagging on a water pipe and an old fishing-net float filled with wadding are just a selection of nesting places that we have recorded. All the sites had one thing in common: they provided a dry, well-insulated home.

There are few reliable differences between species in their nest placement, but most species predominantly favour one of two types of site. Some build a nest on or just below the soil surface, covering it with fine roots, grass and moss (*B. ruderarius, B. hortorum, B. pascuorum, B. sylvarum, B. humilis* and *B. muscorum*). Others make a nest underground, approached by a tunnel varying in length from a few centimetres to more than a metre (*B. terrestris, B. lucorum, B. ruderatus* and *B. lapidarius*). Nest-sites of rarer species are not well known; more information would be useful.

If a small mammal or bird nest has been taken over it may be possible to identify the original owner by examining nest debris (for a useful key to hair and feathers see Day, 1966). Occasionally this is unnecessary: in one nest of *B. hortorum* that we examined the comb was built directly on the decomposing body of a Bank Vole. It is unlikely, although possible, that the queen killed the vole.

One way to acquire a colony is to collect an established nest. Apart from some 'difficult' colonies of *B. terrestris* and *B. muscorum*, British bumblebees are defensive rather than aggressive when their nests are disturbed. Ease of collection therefore depends mainly on nest size and situation. A useful collecting kit includes five or six jam jars with perforated lids, a box or biscuit tin to receive the nest, a pair of thick gloves, trowel, torch, insect net, a pair of forceps and a few specimen tubes with tops. For added confidence a beekeeper's veil and hat are ideal, but not usually necessary.

Evening is the best time for nest collection as most bees are then at home. Before beginning to excavate a subterranean nest it is useful to mark the course of the tunnel with a flexible stick. Gently remove and agitate material covering the nest; this will encourage the occupants to come out to defend it in manageable numbers. It is a simple task to place a tube over each and transfer them to a jar, one after another. Sladen (1912) suggests covering the jar with a card cover, which can be slid aside quickly to let in the next bee. When no more bees appear the comb can be exposed and lifted carefully into a box. It should be kept upright, supported on a bed of material from the nest-site. Collect enough nesting material to allow the bees to re-cover and insulate the nest. Take great care to capture the old queen, who will usually look more worn than any daughter queens that she may have produced. A ball of dry grass left in place of the nest will provide returning bumblebees with somewhere to settle and congregate; they can be collected later the same evening or early the following morning.

As you remove the nest look for the remains of dead queens, which are often to be found amongst nest debris. One may be the original foundress, another her successor, or they may all be unsuccessful intruders. Several species may be found (see p. 14). Nest odour appears to be used by *Psithyrus* females to locate *Bombus* nests, and *Bombus* queens may also use this odour as a cue, allowing some of them to find already established nests that they may be able to take over.

Bumblebees should be returned to the comb as soon as possible after the nest is collected: if you are interested in following the behaviour of individuals, this is a convenient time to mark the bees (see techniques, p. 71). If there is only a little nectar stored in the comb some concentrated sugar solution can be added to empty cells. When choosing a new nest-site make sure that it is well ventilated, protected from rain and direct sun and not exposed to extremes of temperature. Once the nest is in the new site, keep the entrance plugged for a few hours to allow the bees to settle into their new quarters. When the plug is removed the bees that emerge and take off will probably hover facing the nest entrance. This initial phase of orientation lasts a few seconds. Each bumblebee then begins to fly slowly back and forth in front of the nest in an ever-widening pattern, as she inspects and remembers the new nest location and the character of the surroundings. Do not startle bumblebees at this stage or some of them may fly off before learning their way home.

Often the quickest way of obtaining nests is to advertise in your local paper. In addition, the local pest-control officer may be prepared to pass on information about nests reported to him. Many people are only too happy for you to remove nests from their gardens, perhaps forgetting that bumblebees are very useful when it comes to pollinating Runner Beans.

Bumblebees are increasingly under threat from more intensive use of the land, from drainage, and from the spread of modern 'clean' farming practices. Reversal of the decline in their distribution requires the concern and action of all of us. There are a number of steps you can take to encourage bumblebees to nest in gardens and on agricultural land. Shelter in the form of a suitable nest-site, and a *continuous* succession of flowers, are both essential. Therefore always discourage unnecessary tidying-up and so-called improvement of rough land, removal of banks and hedgerows, and the use of herbicides to kill 'weeds' (wild flowers). Derelict land can be made more attractive for bees (and people) by planting a commercially available mixture of wild flower seeds (suppliers, p. 76) which will ensure a food supply throughout the nesting season (March to September). Rotting wood, piles of cut vegetation, mounds of earth and rubble, can all be valuable nesting and hibernation sites. Old stone walls and compost heaps provide potential nest-sites, and nest-boxes can be put out.

Garden plants such as those traditionally grown in a cottage garden provide a good mixture of bumblebee flowers. Most members of the dead-nettle family (Labiatae) are useful (including many of the herbs used in cooking and Salvias and Lavender) as well as Delphiniums, Snapdragons and Honeysuckle. For early spring, when queens have just emerged, Pussy Willow, White Dead-nettle and Flowering Currant provide good sources of forage.

4.2 Making a nest-box

Two types of nest-box are useful: a starter box for nest-founding and small colonies, and another for housing larger nests. The smaller box (internal dimensions about 20 cm long, 10 cm wide and 5 cm deep) should be divided into a nest compartment and an outer chamber. The partition requires a hole (*c.* 2.5 cm) for traffic between the two. On each side wall a similar-diameter hole covered in wire gauze should give adequate ventilation. Make an exit hole, at floor level, in the end wall of the outer chamber. Provide each compartment with a glass or preferably Perspex lid which can be stuck down with tape or otherwise secured. If a gravity feeder is to be used to supply sugar solution a further hole will be needed in the side or end wall of the outer chamber.

A bigger version of the same basic design is suitable for larger colonies (fig. 12). The outer chamber can be relatively smaller, but is still useful as a place to feed the bees and for them to defecate away from the nest. Ventilation holes should be about 5 cm in diameter and are only required in the nest chamber; the degree of ventilation can be varied with a keyhole-type cover. A detachable floor is often useful when housing a large colony and cleaning the box at the end of the season. For outdoor use a runner on either side of the floor will keep the nest off the ground, preventing it getting damp, while a piece of felt carpet underlay covered by a roofing tile or slate will serve as a weatherproof roof. Do not treat wood with preservative or paint as it may upset the bees. New boxes may be more acceptable if they are left outside to weather for several days before being used.

Similar nest-boxes are described in Plowright & Jay (1966) and Alford (1975). Pomeroy & Plowright (1980) give two useful designs, one of which is for a more complex heated nest-box.

4.3 Starting a colony in captivity

In the field, nesting can be encouraged by putting out early in spring nest-boxes containing upholsterer's cotton. (Do not use cotton wool because bumblebees tangle their feet in it.) Other methods of preparing sites in the field are reviewed in Holm (1966) and described in Alford (1975) and Macfarlane & others (1983).

A more reliable way of starting a nest is to catch a queen after she emerges from hibernation. Whenever possible use nest-searching queens (see p. 13). Those carrying

Fig. 12. Bumblebee nest-box (based on a type used by J. B. Free).

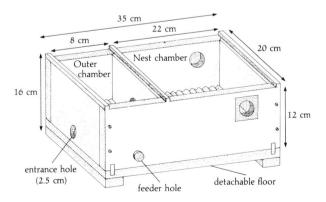

Fig. 13. *B. pratorum* worker taking sugar solution from a small dish.

pollen loads have already founded a colony and are unlikely to begin again. Several methods of proceeding are reviewed in Holm (1966). A method that we have used with some success involves introducing queens into a garden summerhouse, or a small greenhouse. If this can be heated (to 25–30 °C) so much the better. Windows may need to be covered inside with loose-woven cheesecloth or net-curtain material if bees persist in flying against the glass. Flowers are provided as a nectar and pollen supply; for example trays of growing White Dead-nettle, or cut flowers such as Broom *Cytisus scoparius* (L.) and Gorse *Ulex europaeus* L. are both suitable pollen sources. Cut flowers must be changed regularly. Queens will quickly learn to take honey or scented sugar solution (50 : 50 wt sugar/wt water) set out in small shallow dishes; cut ends from plastic egg cartons are quite suitable (see fig. 13). Left relatively undisturbed the queens should become quite accustomed to the unusual surroundings and begin to nest-search, exploring corners and crevices, and even cuffs and trouser legs. If nest-boxes containing upholsterer's cotton are put on shelves and the floor, some queens may begin nesting in them of their own accord.

A less time-consuming method is to confine queens in a small nest-box (see sections 4.2 and 4.4). A ball of pollen dough (see p. 14) the size of a large pea should be provided, together with a supply of sugar solution (to obtain pollen, see techniques, p. 74). Chances of success are increased by putting two or more queens together. Initially they fight, but they usually come to tolerate one another, even if they are of different species (Free & Butler, 1959). Often they cooperate for quite long periods, although frequently one or more is eventually killed.

4.4 How to keep a colony

A starter box can be lined with corrugated cardboard. This will soak up moisture and allow the developing nest to be picked up and transferred to a larger box later on. The exit hole is not needed initially and can be corked.

Fig. 14. A simple gravity feeder for supplying sugar solution.

Bumblebees work hard to keep their nest warm. You can help them by providing insulation (upholsterer's cotton), or by keeping the nest chamber at a temperature of about 30 °C. Warmth will generally improve a colony's chances of developing successfully. Between periods of observation keep the nest dark with a cover.

Sugar solution should be supplied in the outer chamber, either in small plastic dishes or from a gravity feeder. A feeder can be improvised from a syringe, by shortening the nozzle (fig. 14). Avoid spillages – sticky bumblebees

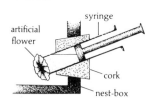

syringe

artificial flower

cork

nest-box

are not enthusiastic about nesting. Make sure the supply of sugar solution does not run out, and always clean the containers and make up fresh solution every couple of days. A very small quantity of clove oil mixed into the solution will help the bees to find and use a new feeder. Honey diluted 1:1 with water is also attractive.

Once a queen has become broody and laid her first eggs, more pollen will be needed. Small pieces of pollen should be placed nearby. These should be replenished as required, or regularly exchanged for fresh material if they are not used. In both pocket-making and pollen-storing species (see p. 15) pollen may be placed in empty cells as these are built or become vacant. In pocket-making species pollen should also be placed directly into the feeding pockets on each larval clump.

Fed in this way a colony can be kept confined. Alternatively, when about 10 workers have hatched they can be allowed out to collect the required nectar and pollen. Once it has begun to grow, the nest can be transferred to a more spacious box.

Bumblebees from indoor boxes will forage outside if a piece of hosepipe, or transparent tube, is passed from the nest entrance out through a window. On the outside, make sure there is an adequate landing platform for easy access to the tube. A coloured surround will help the foragers to locate the correct spot and prevent them wandering in through other windows.

To transfer an established colony to a nest-box follow the guidelines in section 4.1. Avoid dampness and mould from accumulated faeces by lining the outer chamber with absorbent paper, or a little dry soil, which can be replaced periodically.

Finally, try not to disturb the nest unnecessarily. A helpful tip is not to breathe on bumblebees: cultivate the habit, as Sladen (1912) did, of breathing from the side of the mouth when looking at them.

5 Cuckoo bumblebees (*Psithyrus*), parasites and nest associates

5.1 Cuckoo bumblebees

Cuckoo bumblebees, members of the genus *Psithyrus*, look very much like true bumblebees *Bombus*, as we have seen (pl. 4). The resemblance is more than a coincidence. The structural similarities come from shared ancestry: the species of cuckoo bumblebees are thought to have originated from true bumblebees. The similarity of colour patterns may have more immediate ecological significance. Each of the six British species of *Psithyrus* is an inquiline of one or a few species of *Bombus* (see key III), and most of our species show some resemblance to their usual hosts. The function, if any, of this similarity remains unexplained. Are cuckoo bumblebees simply additional members of Müllerian mimicry groups (p. 4) that protect bumblebees from predators?

inquiline: an animal living in the home of another species, and using its food

Cuckoo bumblebees do not work for the colony; they cannot secrete wax and have no pollen baskets. There is no worker caste, all individuals developing into reproductive females or males. The cuckoo larvae are fed and reared by the *Bombus* workers.

In extreme environments, such as the arctic, and probably also at high altitude in some of the mountains of southern Europe, there are *Bombus* species that are capable of behaving just like *Psithyrus*. That is, they do not produce a worker caste of their own, but instead take over nests of another *Bombus* species, the workers of which then rear queens and males for the intruder (Yarrow, 1970; Richards, 1973).

Mated female *Psithyrus* hibernate over winter, emerging rather late in the spring when *Bombus* queens have already established nests. After a period of flower-feeding and ovarian maturation the cuckoo females begin nest-searching, quartering the ground like true bumblebees but searching for established bumblebee nests. When the cuckoo finds the nest of her host species she crawls in through the entrance. The true bumblebees are likely to defend their nest against invaders, and the very thick cuticle of female cuckoo bumblebees is presumably an adaptation that helps protect them against defensive stings. The female cuckoo bumblebee is said to hide among the nest material for a few days, until, perhaps, she begins to smell like a nest-mate and therefore excites less aggression from her hosts. She then emerges into the nest cavity. She may act aggressively towards the host workers, but permits most of them to survive; they will rear her own young. She may kill the host queen. Whether or not she does so seems to vary with her species and may be related to the method of control of queen production by the *Bombus* host (see p. 16). More information is needed on this subject. There are some indications that a *Bombus* queen is more likely to be tolerated by the *Psithyrus* female if she belongs to a 'simple', rather than a 'complex' species (see p. 15).

The *Psithyrus* female often destroys host larvae and eggs and uses the pollen/wax mixture taken from cells of the host to construct egg cells of her own, building them, as *Bombus* does, on top of the cocoons. In them she lays numerous eggs. As her ovaries have more branches (ovarioles) than those of a *Bombus* queen, she can lay more eggs in a batch.

Interestingly, *Psithyrus* species do not show the large differences in tongue length found between some of their *Bombus* hosts. This is presumably because *Psithyrus* females do not compete directly with other bumblebees for nectar, to supply the requirements of their offspring, but instead rely on their *Bombus* hosts to perform this service.

When the cuckoo bumblebees develop into adults and leave the nest they feed lethargically on flowers. The males are particularly slow-moving and obvious, and sometimes give the impression that almost every thistle head is draped with sleepy bumblebees.

As do male true bumblebees, male cuckoo bumblebees patrol particular routes, investigating, at intervals, scent-marked features to which females are thought to come in order to mate. Mated *Psithyrus* females develop their fat bodies and then hibernate in the soil, while males die off before winter.

Cuckoo bumblebees are often locally common and may take over a substantial proportion of *Bombus* colonies. In nest-boxes they can cause severe disappointment, cutting short the colony's development and causing premature production of their own reproductives. Nevertheless, they are interesting bees in their own right and much remains to be discovered about their biology. It is not even certain to what extent each species of *Psithyrus* is limited to its known *Bombus* host species. Does the relationship between the host queen and the cuckoo female vary from one species to another? If so, is it associated with the method of queen production by the *Bombus* host? How does the cuckoo female defend herself and her brood against attack by the host bumblebees?

5.2 Nest associates and parasites

A bumblebee's nest is a rich store of food and cuckoo bumblebees are not the only other animals to take advantage of it. The nest contains a complex community including parasites, predators and large numbers of small insects and mites, of many species: they live in its protected environment, often as scavengers on fragments of wax, pollen and other nutritious material that accumulates there. Many of these nest-mates are tiny and poorly known and there is abundant scope for research on their natural history, and on their impact on the bumblebees' fitness. Here we concentrate on a few of the more conspicuous forms that seem to have a specific association with bumblebees.

One of the most destructive enemies of bumblebee colonies in the wild and in nest-boxes is the Wax Moth *Aphomia sociella* (L.). In summer, the adult moths find and enter bumblebee nests, particularly those built on the ground surface, and lay clusters of eggs. These soon hatch, giving pale larvae which remain in groups, each spinning a silken gallery in which it lives, feeding at first on scraps and rubbish. As the larvae grow they begin to invade the comb, eating cells, food stores and even bumblebee larvae. In this way they quickly destroy the colony, leaving it riddled with their silken galleries. Still moving in a group, the mature larvae then leave the nest, to spin tough winter cocoons in some sheltered place nearby. In these they overwinter. During spring they pupate, to emerge as moths in summer.

Wax Moth caterpillars are not the only caterpillars to be found in bumblebee colonies. A few other species, which appear less frequently and do less damage, are described by Alford (1975). Wax Moth caterpillars, yellowish with olive-green on the back, are fairly distinctive, but for certain identification it would be necessary to rear the adult moths and identify these from Beirne (1954).

Many species of two-winged flies (Order Diptera) are associated with bumblebee nests. Some are generally harmless scavengers. One of the most interesting of these is a large hoverfly (Family Syrphidae) called *Volucella bombylans* (L.). The adult flies, fatter and furrier than most hoverflies, are amazingly good mimics of bumblebees and can easily be mistaken for them in the field, even emitting a similar buzz when caught and raising the middle leg in the typical bumblebee defensive posture. On close inspection they are known to be flies because they have only one pair of wings (bumblebees have two, but often zip the hind wings to the fore wings with a row of hooks) and distinctive feathery antennae (fig. 15). This

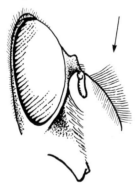

Fig. 15. Antenna of *Volucella bombylans*.

species of hoverfly has several colour forms: one has a white tail and yellow bands, resembling *B. hortorum* and other white-tailed bumblebees, and another is black with a red tail, resembling *B. lapidarius* and *B. ruderarius*. Presumably flies such as *Volucella* are taking advantage of the Müllerian mimicry groups which protect bumblebees from predators (p. 4); experimental evidence is described in Evans & Waldbauer (1982).

A *Volucella* female enters a bumblebee nest and lays her eggs there. A newly killed mature female will sometimes lay her eggs in the killing bottle. This reflex egg-laying probably occurs in nature, allowing females to leave progeny in a nest even if they are killed by bumblebee workers (Sladen, 1912). The legless larvae feed on debris at the bottom of the nest, probably doing no harm to the bumblebees. As in all higher flies the mature larva forms a tough brown puparium; the soft white pupa forms inside the rounded-off, hardened, darkened cuticle of the last larval stage. The puparium overwinters in the nest and the adult hoverfly emerges the following summer. Coloured pictures and descriptions of the adults of *V. bombylans* can be found in Gilbert (1986), and Alford (1975) describes and illustrates the immature stages.

Brachycoma devia (Fallén) of the Family Calliphoridae is a smaller fly, less flamboyant but commoner and more harmful. The adult, looking rather like a House Fly, lays her larvae (rather than eggs) in the clumps of bumblebee larvae in the nest. The fly larvae wait until the bumblebees have finished feeding and spun cocoons in which to pupate. Then they begin to suck out their contents, living as external parasites. At this stage if you open up a pupal cocoon you find, instead of a pupa, a shrinking bumble-bee larva with perhaps three or four little white fly larvae plugged into it, feeding through the cuticle on body fluids. When fully grown each fly larva leaves the cocoon in which it has fed and forms a brown puparium, which may give rise to an adult in a few weeks. There may be several generations a year.

B. devia is very common, parasitising other bees and wasps as well as bumblebees, but it rarely destroys a whole colony. Critical identification is not easy; it is necessary to rear adults and use van Emden's (1954) key.

The conopid flies are distinctive parasites, more likely to attract attention in the field. They are large-headed flies (fig. 16) and many species adopt a very characteristic hunched posture as they sit on flowers, feeding, or ambushing bumblebees. The female fly lays her eggs inside the body cavity of an adult bumblebee, inserting each egg by piercing the bee's body wall with a special structure at the tip of the abdomen. The fly sits on or near

Fig. 16. A conopid fly, *Conops quadrifasciatus* Degeer.

Fig. 17. Anchor-like structure on a conopid egg (*Sicus* species). After Smith (1969).

Fig. 18. The conopid *Physocephala*: third instar larva. After Smith (1969).

trachea: a tube of the respiratory system

a flower and if a bumblebee approaches, the fly shifts around, always facing the bee, perhaps swaying its head from side to side as if taking a fix on the bee. When a bumblebee comes near enough the fly takes to the wing, darts out and grapples with it briefly in flight. The episode is over very quickly, but if you now catch and dissect the bumblebee you will probably find inside it a long, narrow egg with a complex anchor-like or filamentous structure at one end – a conopid egg (fig. 17). The conopid larva that hatches from it (fig. 18) will develop as an internal parasite, eventually growing large enough to fill the host's abdomen. The bumblebee dies, often in her nest, and the fly larva forms a puparium which overwinters within the husk of the host's abdomen, to emerge the following summer.

There are 24 species of conopid flies in Britain and the adults can be named using Smith's (1969) key. Little is known about their biology and distribution in Britain. Observations on conopids in the field or at the nest could make a useful contribution.

A bumblebee's nest is often alive with tiny mites and the bees themselves are often found to carry numerous mites, especially lodged at the back of the thorax. Identifying mites is a job for an expert; therefore they are not easy animals to work on, although much remains to be discovered about them. One of the commonest species found on foraging adult bumblebees is *Parasitus fucorum* (De Geer) (fig. 19). Its young stages develop, probably as scavengers, in bumblebee nests. When nearly mature the mites attach themselves to adult bumblebees, particularly young queens. In this way they remain with the queen throughout the winter and can invade her new nest when she establishes it in spring. If you examine a few mites from a bumblebee's thorax, mounting them on a microscope slide and using a compound microscope, you may see an even smaller mite that lives on them, a bizarre tortoise-like mite with huge claws: *Scutacarus acarorum* (Goeze) (fig. 20). Mites of another species are sometimes found inhabiting the respiratory system of bumblebees, feeding on the bumblebee's blood through the wall of the trachea. These and many other mites are described and illustrated by Alford (1975).

One of the most important and unusual bumblebee parasites is a microscopic roundworm, or nematode, *Sphaerularia bombi* Dufour. This infects only queens, but it can seriously disrupt the behaviour and physiology of its hosts, and an understanding of its effects is necessary for the interpretation of field observations on queen bumblebees. A proportion of the queens caught in spring contain in the abdomen a white, bobbly, sausage-shaped

Fig. 19. *Parasitus* species deutonymph.

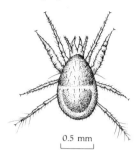

0.5 mm

corpora allata: small secretory organs behind the brain

structure about 10–20 millimetres long (fig. 21). This is an adult female roundworm – or rather it is the reproductive system of the worm, turned inside out, with the rest of the worm attached as a tiny strand at one end. It produces large numbers of eggs which are released into the blood of the bumblebee. Inside each, a roundworm larva develops through its first two stages. In the third stage it hatches; examination of the bumblebee's blood under a compound microscope at this time reveals thousands of larvae as little white strands about 1 millimetre long. From the blood these larvae move into the gut and reproductive system and eventually reach the outside world, often in the bumblebee's faeces.

A surprising feature of this parasite's life history is that it centres not on the bumblebee's nest but on the hibernation site. Here mated adult worms infect new queens when these arrive and burrow into the soil at the beginning of winter. Within the infected queen in spring the female roundworm grows, turns its reproductive system inside out, and starts releasing eggs. The effect on the host is remarkable. In a healthy queen in spring, the corpora allata release a hormone in the presence of which the ovaries develop. When this happens the queen begins to search for a nest-site and establish a nest. In a parasitised queen the roundworm somehow prevents the development of the bee's corpora allata: the ovaries fail to develop and the queen does not search for a nest-site and establish a nest, or load her pollen baskets with pollen. Instead she forages for herself alone, in a desultory way, and may return to the hibernation site. Here numbers of parasitised queens may spend their time.

Fig. 20. *Scutacarus acarorum*: a mite that lives on mites that live on bumblebees.

Fig. 21. *Sphaerularia bombi*: a nematode parasite of bumblebees.

0.1 mm

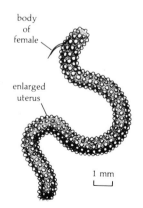

body of female

enlarged uterus

1 mm

When worm larvae are discharged in their faeces the soil
of the hibernation site becomes infected, and it is here
that the worms develop, mate and infect new queens as
these arrive to hibernate in autumn. The life history of *S.
bombi* is described and illustrated by Poinar & van der
Laan (1972) and Alford (1975).

In early spring there may be no obvious behavioural
differences between infected and healthy queens. However, the healthy individuals soon begin establishing
colonies, and by summer most of these queens will be
confined to their nests; the majority of queens still seen at
flowers will be those carrying the roundworm.

5.3 Predators

Bumblebees have many parasites but few predators,
perhaps because of their sting. We have seen that con-
vergence in colour pattern has been interpreted as Müllerian mimicry (p. 4). A system like this will give protection
only against predators that hunt by sight, and the accu-
racy of the mimetic patterns implicates predators with
good visual acuity. Apart from spiders, most bumblebee
predators are vertebrates. Spotted Flycatchers *Muscicapa
striata* destroy bumblebees' stings by wiping the insects
against a branch (Davies, 1977). Further south in Europe,
Bee-eaters *Merops apiaster* can also remove bees' stings.
Shrikes, particularly the Red-backed Shrike *Lanius col-
lurio*, collect bumblebees and impale them, along with
other prey, on the thorns of a 'larder' bush. Badgers *Meles
meles* will dig out nests and feed on their contents. In
Iceland bumblebees and their brood sometimes form a
large part of the diet of Mink *Mustela vison* (see Prŷs-Jones,
Ólafsson & Kristjánsson, 1981). Other than man, the
vertebrates causing the most trouble for bumblebees are
probably small mammals. These may invade nests and
destroy them; they probably eat the bees and larvae. But
of course bumblebees also benefit from small mammals,
as their abandoned nests provide the sites for many
bumblebee colonies.

6 Foraging behaviour

6.1 Economics of foraging

In collaboration with ecologists, true bumblebees have played a large part in the development of 'optimal foraging theory'. A book by Krebs & Davies (1981) gives a good introduction to this method of studying behaviour. Briefly, optimal foraging theory consists of a framework of economic ideas: these enable the behaviour of a real bee to be compared with the behaviour that might be expected if the bee were trying to achieve a particular aim. It is often suggested that the 'aim' of a foraging worker is to maximise her rate of gain of some necessary 'currency' (usually taken to be energy), given certain constraints. A constraint might be, say, the necessity to sample the available flower types, or the requirement for water or a particular nutrient.

By permitting the incorporation of mathematical ideas, this method of considering behaviour 'dignifies' bumblebee natural history with the status of theoretical ecology. However, it is important to bear in mind that this mathematical treatment of biological systems requires simplifying assumptions, and the selection of assumptions that are at once realistic and productive requires, perhaps, a deeper understanding of bumblebee biology than is yet available. We should not underestimate the extent to which major theoretical advances will depend on patient observational studies of natural history. More observations of the type outlined below should help us gain a better understanding of the ways in which bumblebees enhance their foraging efficiency.

The energetic costs of foraging can be estimated from the work Heinrich (1979) has done on bumblebee energetics. Insects can only fly if their flight muscles (which constitute most of the thorax) are warm enough. Bumblebees require a higher temperature than most insects: the thorax is normally maintained at between 30 and 40 °C during flight, and if it cools below 27 °C the bee can only crawl. Despite this requirement bumblebees can often be seen flying at air temperatures well below this. They can do so because of their ability to generate and retain heat. As in all insects, the muscular flight motor is not perfectly efficient, and only about 20% of its power output does useful work; the rest goes as heat, which warms the thorax during flight. So a bee that keeps flying keeps warm.

In preparation for flight, and in order to incubate a brood, bumblebees can warm up by shivering. This involves repeatedly contracting the flight muscles, while functionally uncoupling them from the wings. No useful work is done, but heat is produced.

Surprisingly, a bumblebee's flight muscles also appear to be able to generate heat without contracting. This seems to be achieved by an energy-releasing biochemical cycle (a substrate cycle) under the bee's control (Newsholme & others, 1972). The mechanism probably enables bumblebees to warm up, or at least reduce their rate of cooling, between periods of flight. Substrate cycling is a 'cheaper' means of heat generation than shivering because none of the energy is wasted in unused muscular contraction. Recently we measured the activity of the enzyme required for this cycle (fructose bisphosphatase) in four common British bumblebee species (*B. pascuorum*, *B. terrestris*, *B. hortorum* and *B. lapidarius*), and found much the highest values in *B. lapidarius* (Prŷs-Jones & Crabtree, 1983, and table 4). Remember that *B. lapidarius* tends to specialise in foraging on massed flowers, such as composites, in which individual florets are often nectar-poor but the clustered arrangement allows a bee to probe many flowers between flights. By enabling the bees to keep warm cheaply, high enzyme activity may make foraging on such flowers more profitable for *B. lapidarius* than it is for other bumblebee species which must rely more on shivering in order to keep warm enough to fly on to the next flower. Such physiological differences between species may account for a number of differences in foraging behaviour and deserve further study.

Table 4. *Foraging behaviour and the activity of fructose bisphosphatase in the flight muscles*

Species	Fructose bisphosphatase activity (μmol min^{-1} g^{-1} muscle, mean ± standard error)[a]	Proportion of visits to massed flower arrangements[b]
B. lapidarius	131 ± 7 (8)	0.54 (210)
B. lucorum	80 ± 16 (5)	0.39 (84)
B. pratorum	73 ± 10 (13)	0.19 (177)
B. terrestris	59 ± 13 (7)	0.38 (188)
B. pascuorum	45 + 6 (20)	0.18 (254)
B. hortorum	23 ± 1 (11)	0.07 (159)

Correlation coefficient, $r = 0.88$, df = 5, $P < 0.02$

[a] Based on data supplied by B. Crabtree (summarised in Newsholme & others, 1972), and on Prŷs-Jones & Crabtree (1983). Numbers in brackets are sample size.
[b] From Prŷs-Jones (1986). Numbers in brackets are sample size.

Although substrate cycling is cheaper than shivering, the fuel to power both systems is costly. Insulating body hair helps bumblebees economise by reducing their rate of loss of heat, and in cool weather they often use supplementary solar heating, basking on sunny surfaces. Sometimes they will even flatten themselves against the warm, sunlit jersey or sock of an observer.

This ability to generate a high body temperature enables bumblebees to fly in cold weather and to maintain a steady high temperature in the nest. It permits them to forage very early in the morning and late in the evening, when there is little competition from other flower-visiting insects (see p. 38 for implications regarding forager numbers at various times of day) and it enables them to thrive at high latitudes and at high altitudes. Although they can regulate cooling rates to some extent, by controlling the flow of warm blood past the hairless 'heat window' on the lower surface of the abdomen (Heinrich, 1979), a sturdy, furry flying machine the size of a bumblebee will always be above ambient temperature when active, and overheating is probably a serious problem. Bumblebees often show a lull in flower-visiting activity in the hottest part of a sunny day, and at low latitudes they are commonest in cool, mountainous regions.

Generation of a high body temperature accounts for most of the energetic cost of activity. By measuring the rates of oxygen consumption of flying bumblebees in the laboratory, Heinrich (1975) has shown that flight costs a bumblebee about 0.44 watts per gram body weight, or about 0.07 watts for a bumblebee weighing 150 milligrams. Crawling is cheaper, the exact cost depending on the temperature of the thorax and the air. Clearly, in order to estimate a bumblebee's foraging costs one needs to know what proportion of its time is spent on the wing; for this a cumulative stopwatch will help. A bumblebee crawling slowly over the massed inflorescences of Goldenrod *Solidago* species allows its thorax to cool down, and so can cut costs. One foraging rapidly, or pausing briefly between short flights, needs to keep its thorax warm so that it can fly again without delay, and so must expend more energy.

In this way it is possible to estimate a bumblebee's expenses while it is working a patch of flowers. If one adds to these the costs of flying to and from the nest, again calculated on the basis of observed flight times, one gets the overall cost of a return foraging trip from the nest to the flowers and back.

Profits to be set against these costs can be computed from the number of flowers visited per trip and the mean reward per flower. However, it is not easy to follow a bumblebee for an entire trip to count its flower visits. Instead, one can record the rate of flower visitation (from timings of, say, 10 or 20 visits), and estimate the duration of a whole foraging trip by noting the times when marked individuals (technique, p. 71) are seen at the foraging patch, or when they are seen to enter or leave the nest; thus the number of flowers visited per trip can be estimated.

At this stage it is worth making a point the significance of which is often overlooked. A female bumblebee must transport each load to her nest (she is a 'central place' forager). As a result, when nectar is abundant she may spend quite a small proportion of a foraging trip actually *on* flowers compared with time spent travelling to and from the colony and depositing the load. Conversely, when nectar is scarce (often in the middle of the day), a large proportion of her time will be spent on flowers. This has paradoxical consequences. First, if one makes counts of the number of bees on flowers at various times, numbers of foragers may appear to increase as resources decrease. Second, if one attempted to estimate the extent of competition between species just by counting bees on flowers, one would seriously overestimate the contribution of times when large numbers of bees are present but little food is available to any of the foragers. For example, the extent to which bumblebees *Bombus* experience competition from honeybees *Apis* for nectar would almost certainly be overestimated. Both forage during the middle of the day, when the amount of nectar available is often quite small. But bumblebees also forage early in the morning, late in the evening and under more adverse weather conditions than honeybees – times when nectar is often relatively abundant. They may therefore gather the majority of their requirements at times when honeybees are not present.

The need to transport each stomachful of nectar to the nest also has implications that relate to the volume and concentration of nectar per flower. The decisions that enable a forager to gather the maximum amount of sugar per unit time for her nest may often depend more on nectar volume and concentration than on the amount of sugar per flower. A bee's honeystomach holds only a limited volume of nectar. The more concentrated that nectar is, the more sugar the nest gains from each load. Foraging a given distance (travel time) from the nest a bumblebee may be able to bring home a greater weight of sugar per unit time by visiting flowers containing concentrated nectar, than by visiting flowers supplying larger volumes of more dilute nectar (even though the latter contain an equal or *greater* weight of sugar per flower). Alternatively, the choice may be between flowers close to the nest and others at a distance. In this case foragers may make a greater rate of gain of sugar to the colony by visiting the closer flowers, even if these provide more dilute and/or smaller amounts of nectar per flower (Prŷs-Jones, 1982).

Other less obvious features may be important too. Nectar is not *just* an energy source: unlike honeybees, which will collect water on its own, bumblebees must achieve water balance for themselves and their brood entirely from the water contained in nectar. What compromises are involved so as to balance the need for energy with the requirement for water? So far, this important point has been overlooked when considering queen and worker foraging, both in optimal foraging models and in field studies. If bumblebee larvae do not thrive on highly concentrated nectar, as is the case with honeybee larvae, foragers may sometimes select lower-concentration nectars than those which would be most profitable energetically. In contrast, male bumblebees forage only for themselves, and an elegant experimental study by Bertsch (1984) has shown that they may gain water, from flight metabolism and from nectar, faster than they can lose it. Bees' activity patterns may sometimes be structured by the need to discharge excess water.

The energetic reward per flower can be calculated from the volume and concentration of the nectar in each, on the assumption that all the solutes in nectar are sugars (which is almost, but not quite, true). Nectar volume can be measured by allowing the nectar to run up into a microcapillary tube, and measuring the length of the nectar column (technique, p. 73). From such measurements made on, say, 10 or 20 flowers, it is possible to calculate the mean weight of sugar per flower and so discover how much sugar a bee acquires during her whole foraging trip. Variability in the amount of sugar per flower is also important: the same mean weight of sugar per flower may be based on, for example, one full flower in 10, or 10 partly full flowers. If a bee samples only five flowers before deciding whether to stay or leave, it will make a different profit, and may therefore behave differently in the two cases.

A word of caution is needed here. Close observation will probably reveal that bumblebees are selective in the flowers they visit, perhaps choosing flowers of a particular age, or in a particular position on each plant or inflorescence. As far as possible, nectar samples should be taken from flowers chosen on the same basis. Even then, sampling may underestimate the quantity of sugar a bee can collect, because bumblebees may be avoiding recently visited (and therefore empty) flowers in a way that an observer cannot do.

Measurements of nectar quantity and timings of bumblebee visits must be done quickly, because both may change markedly from hour to hour and from day to day. Nectar content changes as rates of secretion, and rates of removal by flower visitors, vary with the weather. Nectar solute concentration changes with ambient relative humidity, especially in open flowers, where the nectar may become concentrated and viscous by evaporation in dry air (Corbet, Willmer & others, 1979; Corbet, Unwin & Prŷs-Jones, 1979). Bee visiting patterns, and the time taken to empty each flower, will also change through the day, as weather influences the bees' behaviour directly, and also influences the amounts and quality of nectar per flower (see Willmer, 1983).

A nectar-collecting bumblebee usually leaves the nest carrying only a small reserve of nectar, so that the nectar she carries in her honeystomach when she returns represents the net profit from her foraging trip. The honeystomach, a cuticle-lined swelling in the foregut, lies in the front of the abdomen (fig. 22). A bumblebee fills (or nearly fills) it with nectar when she is foraging, flies back to the nest, and regurgitates its contents into an empty pupal cell or specially constructed wax cell. In British bumblebees the honeystomach of a worker holds between about 60 and 200 microlitres of fluid, depending on the size of the bee. When it is full, a simple dissection reveals the honeystomach as a clear, spherical bag of nectar (technique, p. 72). If the oesophagus has been cut by first removing the bee's head, the whole honeystomach can be removed from the abdomen with a pair of forceps. If it is punctured the nectar flows out, and the volume and concentration can be measured. In this way the load can be estimated. An alternative technique, preferable because it need not damage the bee, is to anaesthetise the bee (technique, p. 71), unfold the tongue, and press gently on the tip of the abdomen using one's thumbnail (to avoid the sting). The honeystomach contents will be regurgitated and can be collected into a microcapillary tube for measurement of volume and concentration (technique, p. 73).

Using these techniques it should be possible to explore the energetic profitability of bumblebee foraging in different circumstances, and to see how profitability is influenced by, say, the distance of the flower patch from the nest; or the distance apart of flowers in a clump; or the presence of honeybees.

Unlike honeybees, which use information received

Fig. 22. *B. terrestris* worker dissected to show the honeystomach.

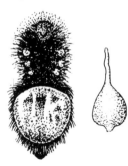

from other foragers, bumblebees learn where to forage by their own initiative. As mentioned above, tongue length varies between *Bombus* species and influences which flowers are visited for nectar. Similar patterns are found within species: larger workers with longer tongues learn to visit a slightly different range of flowers than their smaller, shorter-tongued sisters (table 5).

By timing the flower visits'of newly emerged and more experienced workers, Heinrich (1976) has shown how important learning is as a component of successful foraging. On complicated flowers such as Monkshood *Aconitum*, true bumblebees take some time to learn the best way of acquiring nectar, and increase their foraging efficiency very much by doing so. Learning is important in another sense. An experienced bumblebee working a familiar and productive patch of flowers may adopt a regular foraging route, which she follows repeatedly with only minor variations (Manning, 1956). Presumably the bee leaves time between circuits for fresh secretion to replenish the nectar in the flower. This systematic visiting pattern must help to ensure that she does not revisit the flowers she has just emptied.

Other systematic patterns may serve the same function. Bumblebees working flowers arranged in vertical spikes usually work upwards on a spike, flying downwards between plants to start near the bottom of the next spike. This is easy to confirm by counting the proportion

Table 5. *Tongue length and foraging behaviour within species*

Species and size of worker	Tongue length (mm, mean ± standard error)[a]	Corolla length (mm, mean ± standard error)[b]
B. terrestris		
small	6.9 ± 0.1 (11)	5.6 ± 0.3 (40)
medium	8.5 ± 0.2 (15)	6.3 ± 0.2 (112)
large	9.3 ± 0.1 (9)	7.7 ± 0.4 (16)
B. pratorum		
small	6.2 ± 0.2 (8)	6.9 ± 1.3 (9)
medium	7.3 ± 0.1 (9)	7.1 ± 0.4 (76)
large	7.8 ± 0.8 (9)	9.0 ± 1.0 (15)
B. pascuorum		
small	6.9 ± 0.1 (6)	7.3 ± 0.4 (23)
medium	8.4 ± 0.1 (15)	8.0 ± 0.2 (203)
large	10.1 ± 0.2 (10)	8.6 ± 0.3 (125)

[a] Numbers in brackets are sample size.
[b] The average weighted by frequency of visitation (% × corolla length/100). Based on flower visits for nectar, and nectar + pollen. Numbers in brackets are sample size.
From Prŷs-Jones (1982).

of flower-to-flower movements, on a spike or between spikes, that are upwards, downwards or level. There has been much discussion about the significance of this habit to the bees; one possibility is considered in Krebs & Davies (1981), and others are discussed by Corbet & others (1981). It may sometimes be of adaptive significance to the flowers too, favouring cross-pollination. In species such as Rosebay Willowherb *Chamerion angustifolium* (L.), whose flowers open in order from the bottom upwards, ripening their anthers before their stigmas, the lower flowers will be effectively female and the upper ones effectively male. The upwards directionality of the bumblebees will therefore mean that a bee, arriving newly dusted with pollen from another plant, deposits this on the ripe stigmas of the lower flowers before picking up a fresh load of pollen from the anthers of the upper flowers, and transferring this to another plant.

Flower scent and colour may provide recognisable cues which result in further patterns of foraging behaviour. A recently emptied flower may smell less strongly than a full one, and thereby save the bee the trouble of alighting. This possibility has been explored for White Clover *Trifolium repens* L. (Heinrich, 1979), but it remains to be tested for other species. Colour changes may provide similar information; for example petals of young flowers of Horse-chestnut *Aesculus hippocastanum* L. are marked with yellow, whereas in old flowers the marks are red.

On some flower visits a bumblebee collects nectar only. In such cases her pollen baskets may be empty, or she may carry persistent pollen masses left over from an earlier trip. Often she will collect both nectar and pollen, probing with her tongue at the base of the flower, becoming dusted with pollen meanwhile, and periodically hovering or pausing on a flower to groom her body hairs and comb the resulting pollen into the pollen baskets on her hind legs. Sometimes a bee collects pollen alone, even when the flower type produces nectar; species differ in the frequency with which they do this (table 1). *B. lucorum* does so often; the habit is less common among the other species, and *B. hortorum*, at the opposite extreme, nearly always collects nectar and pollen together when pollen-gathering. In addition, *B. pratorum* and *B. hortorum*, both of which have a short life cycle, collect pollen on a much higher percentage of flower visits than other common species (table 1). With information of this type patterns of ecological differences between species begin to emerge (fig. 23). In fig. 23 the pattern presumably reflects colony demands on the forager population, resulting from species differences in colony size and the length of the colony cycle, and differences in individual abilities, which vary with tongue length and thermoregulatory efficiency.

Some flowers lack nectar, and pollen is the only resource available; Meadowsweet *Filipendula ulmaria* (L.) Maxim., Broom *Cytisus scoparius* and some St John's Worts *Hypericum* species are examples. A pollen-collecting bumblebee may scramble over the anthers, coating her body in pollen which is later groomed off; or she may dislodge the pollen by vibration, emitting a distinctive high-pitched buzz. This latter method is frequently used when visiting flowers with tubular anthers with a hole at one end, such as Woody Nightshade *Solanum dulcamara* L. Tomato flowers have anthers like this too, and commercial growers sometimes use a vibrating 'electric bee' to assist hand pollination.

Even when a bumblebee does not take both pollen and nectar from the same flower, she may collect both on the same trip. In such cases the forager, though probing a flower for nectar only, will be seen to carry pollen loads on her legs. The presence of such loads does not necessarily mean she is collecting pollen this trip – she may have failed to unload her baskets after an earlier trip – but the absence of pollen loads and pollen-collecting behaviour does indicate that a bumblebee is collecting nectar alone.

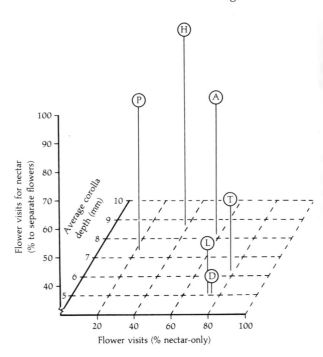

Fig. 23. Patterns of flower-visiting behaviour (see text). Letters indicate species: *B. hortorum* (H), *B. pratorum* (P), *B. pascuorum* (A), *B. terrestris* (T), *B. lucorum* (L) and *B. lapidarius* (D). Based on information collected throughout the life cycle of each species. From Prŷs-Jones (1982).

Pollen collection is dictated partly by the needs of the nest, but the time at which flowers release their pollen must be important too. The splitting open of the anthers depends critically on the weather. A species of flower that releases its pollen early in the morning on fine days, may release it at quite a different time of day in bad weather.

Some flowers, such as Hollyhocks *Alcea rosea* L., produce pollen that seems to be unacceptable to some bees. Further study of this is needed. In some circumstances it could be adaptive for a plant to produce pollen of this kind. Instead of grooming it away to their pollen baskets, bumblebees leave the pollen for some time, daubed on the body hair, where it may contact a stigma before they eventually groom it off and reject it, kicking it off the ends of their legs (fig. 24).

Fig. 24. *B. pascuorum* queen grooming.

By examining a bee's pollen loads it is possible to make an (incomplete) list of the flowers she has been visiting. When the pollen has a characteristic colour, like the blue of Viper's Bugloss *Echium vulgare* L. or the orange of Mullein *Verbascum* species, this can be done on sight, without disturbing the bee; the colours of various pollens, as seen in honeybee loads, are illustrated by Hodges (1974). More usually the pollen grains must be examined under a compound microscope (technique, p. 75), when their elaborate sculptured shapes (fig. 25) make it possible to identify them with the aid of a key (Moore & Webb, 1978; Sawyer, 1981), or, more conveniently, by comparison with pollen samples collected from flowers known to be available to the bees.

If one finds a nest it is possible (with practice) to identify the almost indestructible husks of the pollen grains that have been eaten and egested by the larvae. Just before pupation each larva empties its gut inside its newly spun pupal cocoon. Traces of this larval faecal material can be scraped from within the empty cocoons and the pollen grain husks can be identified (Brian, 1951; Yalden, 1982). If you can 'read' the history of the colony, recognising successive batches of cocoons from their relative positions, it may be possible to reconstruct the seasonal succession of pollen sources. Work of this type is valuable in that it can help to show which plants are important in maintaining local bumblebee populations.

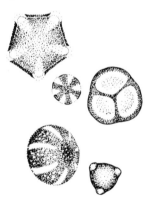

Fig. 25. Pollen grains from some bumblebee-visited plant species.

Bumblebees, like most social bees, are generalists – nearly all British species will visit a wide range of flower species. This is fortunate for us because it means that bumblebees readily forage in crops and gardens, even where the native flowers are suppressed as weeds and replaced by species introduced from all over the world. With the possible exception of the handsome *B. monticola*, which inhabits moorland where *Vaccinium* species

PLATE 1

1
Bombus lucorum ♀

2
B. lucorum ♂

3
B. terrestris ♀

4
B. terrestris ♀

5
B. hortorum ♀

6
B. jonellus ♀

7
B. jonellus ♂

8
B. ruderatus ♀
(pale)

9
B. ruderatus ♀
(dark)

10
B. ruderatus ♀
(intermediate)

PLATE 2

1
Bombus lapidarius ♀

2
B. lapidarius ♂

3
B. ruderarius ♀

4
B. ruderarius ♂

5
B. pratorum ♀

6
B. pratorum ♂

7
B. sylvarum ♀

8
B. monticola ♀

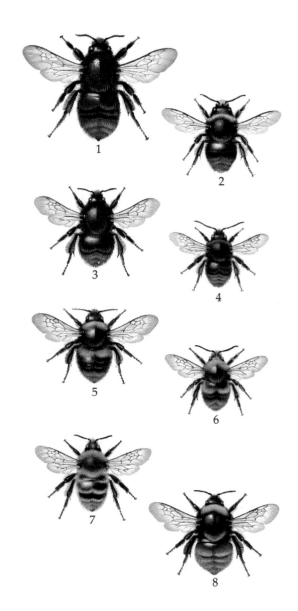

PLATE 3

1
Bombus soroeensis ♀

2
B. soroeensis ♂

3
B. distinguendus ♀

4
B. muscorum ♀

5
B. pascuorum ♀

6
B. pascuorum ♀

7
B. pascuorum ♀

8
B. humilis ♀

9
B. subterraneus ♀

10
B. subterraneus ♂

PLATE 4

1
Psithyrus rupestris ♀

2
P. rupestris ♂

3
P. sylvestris ♀

4
P. sylvestris ♂

5
P. bohemicus ♀

6
P. bohemicus ♂

7
P. vestalis ♀

8
P. vestalis ♂

9
P. barbutellus ♀

10
P. campestris ♀

11
P. campestris ♂
(dark)

12
P. campestris ♂
(light)

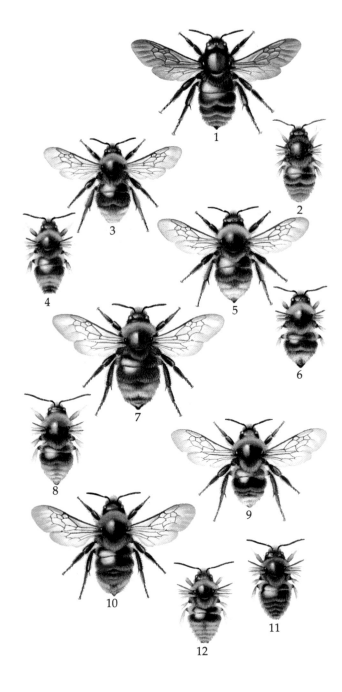

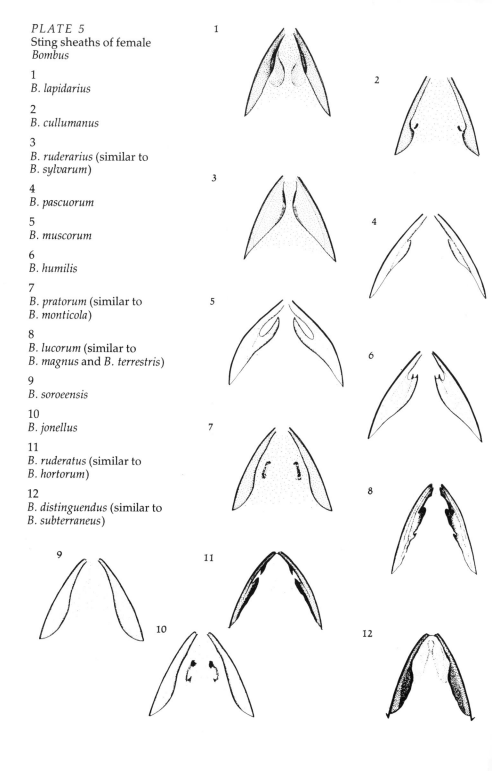

PLATE 5
Sting sheaths of female
Bombus

1
B. lapidarius

2
B. cullumanus

3
B. ruderarius (similar to
B. sylvarum)

4
B. pascuorum

5
B. muscorum

6
B. humilis

7
B. pratorum (similar to
B. monticola)

8
B. lucorum (similar to
B. magnus and *B. terrestris*)

9
B. soroeensis

10
B. jonellus

11
B. ruderatus (similar to
B. hortorum)

12
B. distinguendus (similar to
B. subterraneus)

PLATE 6

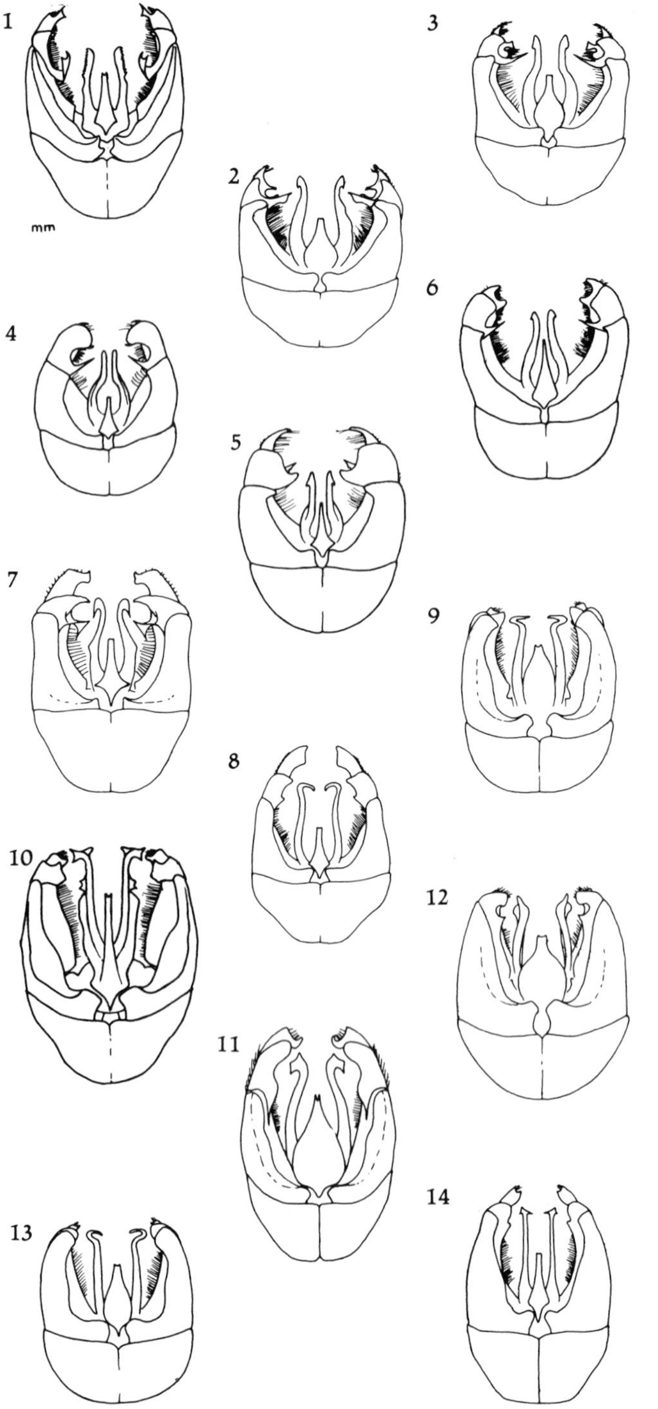

Genital capsules of male
Bombus

1
B. hortorum
(similar to *B. ruderatus*)

2
B. ruderarius

3
B. sylvarum

4
B. pascuorum

5
B. humilis

6
B. muscorum

7
B. pomorum

8
B. cullumanus

9
B. jonellus
(similar to 13)

10
B. distinguendus
(similar to *B. subterraneus*)

11
B. soroeensis

12
B. terrestris
(similar to *B. lucorum* and
B. magnus)

13
B. pratorum
(similar to *B. monticola*)

14
B. lapidarius

PLATE 7

Callosities on the last (6th)
ventral plate of female
Psithyrus

1
P. rupestris

2
P. sylvestris

3
P. campestris

4
P. barbutellus

5
P. vestalis

6
P. bohemicus

1

2

3

4

5

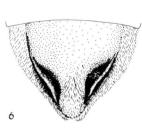

6

PLATE 8

Genital capsules of male
Psithyrus

1
P. campestris

2
P. rupestris

3
P. sylvestris

4
P. bohemicus

5
P. barbutellus

6
P. vestalis

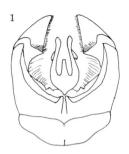

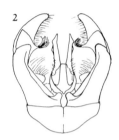

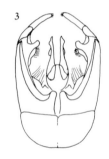

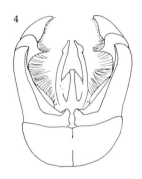

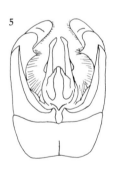

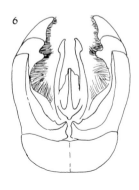

(Bilberry, Cowberry, Cranberry) grow, our bumblebees do not appear to depend on particular plant species. Do any of our plant species depend on bumblebees for pollination? We may speculate that among the flowers best adapted for pollination by bees of this shape and size are members of the mint family (Labiatae), particularly White Dead-nettle; and flowers such as Common Toadflax *Linaria vulgaris* Mill. require a bumblebee's strength to open the lips of the flower, and the long tongue of *B. hortorum* to reach the nectar in the spur.

6.2 Studying foraging behaviour and pollination

If we are to understand the causes and the potential consequences of the decline of bumblebees in Britain and how they can be remedied, we need more information on the importance of particular flower species for the various species of bumblebee, and on the importance of the bumblebee species as pollinators of both wild flowers and crops.

We have seen that useful information on the various plant species used by bees as pollen sources can be gained from analysis of pollen loads and faecal material from nests. Unfortunately there is no corresponding way of unravelling the seasonal history of a colony's nectar collection; there is no substitute here for direct observation. As we have outlined, evaluating the importance of the nectar source for bees is not as straightforward as it seems. One problem is that the relative value of different flowers changes through the day, with weather-related changes in the concentration and volume of the nectar available in them. This means that a thorough investigation of flower usage in a particular locality at a particular time should really span the whole foraging period of a day (or, better still, several days). Because bumblebees can forage at low ambient temperatures, this may mean starting early (perhaps as early as 4 a.m. in summer) and continuing late (perhaps after 10 p.m.).

An all-day session of this kind can give useful results, particularly if combined with studies of nectar availability (see p. 73) and microclimate (p. 77), but it is best done by a group of people, and needs careful planning beforehand. Counts are made in a standard way at regular intervals of, say, 1½–2 hours through the day. They usually involve making a 'bee walk' along a pre-selected route, often a hedgerow or bank providing a defined strip of flowers perhaps 1–2 metres wide and up to about 100 metres long, and recording, for each bee seen visiting a flower, the species of flower, species, sex and caste (whether queen or worker) of bee, and whether the bee is

taking nectar, pollen, or both. Alternatively, when bees
are very abundant, a bee count might involve spot counts
of the numbers of bees active at a given time within, say,
five quadrats; or counts of the numbers entering (or
leaving) a quadrat during a period of, say, 10 minutes.
The interpretation of spot counts highlights the second
problem in a study of this kind, in that a high count may
mean one of two things. It may mean that the flowers
have attracted a large number of bumblebees because
nectar is abundant. Alternatively, it may mean that each
bee is having to spend a long time in the patch because
each flower contains very little nectar and a bee must visit
many flowers to fill its honeystomach. To distinguish
between these two possibilities one requires information
on nectar availability and foraging rate.

An obvious prerequisite for work of this kind is that
every observer should be able to recognise the species of
flowers and the species, sex and caste of the bumblebees,
without taking specimens. This requires some work
beforehand. The plates and keys in chapter 7 of this book
should enable bumblebees to be named. It is sometimes
useful to take into the field a named reference collection
of local bumblebee species pinned out in a clear sandwich
box (see p. 71). Flowers can be named with the aid of a
book such as Clapham, Tutin & Warburg (1981), Keble
Martin (1982) or McClintock & Fitter (1982).

Studies of this kind are particularly valuable if they
relate to crop plants, or wild plants of species that might
be encouraged on waste land or road verges; and if they
relate to seasons (early spring and the 'June gap') when
nectar can be in critically short supply.

If particular species of bumblebee continue to decline
will crops and wild flowers suffer reduced pollination? As
mentioned above, to explore the role of bees for particular
plants is worth while, especially if those plants are species
of importance to agriculture, horticulture or conservation. One way to see whether bee pollination influences
seed set is to enclose flowers, from the bud stage
onwards, in loose bags of petticoat netting or bridal
veiling, of mesh fine enough to exclude bees but not fine
enough to have serious effects on the flowers' microclimate. Control flowers are tagged at the same time and left
exposed to pollinators. After a period of perhaps 3–10
days it should be possible to see whether or not seed is
setting in the bagged and exposed flowers. The experi-
ment should be left longer if the seeds are to be allowed to
mature, and be counted and weighed. If bagging substan-
tially reduces seed set, bees, or other insects too large to
get through the mesh, may be significant pollinators. If
not, the plant may need no pollination, or it may be

self-pollinated or pollinated by smaller insects or by the wind.

If bagged flowers set no seed, one way to see which visitors are effective pollinators is to bag a flower until it is fully open, then remove the bag and watch patiently until the flower has been visited once (or twice, or three times) by the suspected pollinator, then re-bag it at once and later score seed set. Another, more direct way to get information is to examine the stigma with a lens: it may be possible to see whether or not pollen is present on it. A bumblebee visit may result in the appearance of pollen on a hitherto pollen-free stigma. If the stigma is sampled at once, the presence of pollen can be checked microscopically (technique, p. 76); but if the flower is bagged and left for a few hours, it may be possible to show that the pollen has germinated, forming a pollen tube (technique, p. 76), and was therefore viable pollen of the same species.

Other approaches involve discovering the type of pollen being carried by flower-visiting bumblebees. One useful method is to wash the bees in alcohol, then filter out the grains and examine them (technique, p. 75). Another method involves the 'Sellotape peel' technique (p. 75) to map the position of pollen of different species on the bee's body hair. This may help to identify which parts of a bee contact the stigma of each flower species that it visits.

Many other aspects of foraging offer scope for further work. The possibility that pollen from certain plants is rejected by certain bumblebee species (p. 44), and the way bees select flowers to visit within a patch, both need much more investigation. If each flower is marked, mapped or collected after it is visited, it may be possible to see whether the bees are preferentially visiting, say, the larger flowers; or the lower flowers; or those at a particular stage of flowering; or those with or without other insects in them, such as thrips or beetle larvae. Do flowers of the selected type contain more nectar than the òthers? The possibility that individual bees have regular foraging routes, perhaps visited day after day, is also worth further investigation, using bumblebees that have been marked so that they can be recognised individually (technique, p. 71). In a study of this kind it is important for the observer to sit quietly to avoid disturbing the bees; it may take them 10 minutes or so to return to their normal foraging behaviour after an observer's arrival.

Is there any evidence for positive or negative interactions between bumblebees of the same or different species? Brian (1957) has suggested that bumblebees are more likely to approach a foraging site if other bumblebees are already there. She has also suggested that some bumblebees avoid other species: *B. pascuorum*, in particular, seems likely to leave a foraging patch when other species arrive. Is there a hierarchy of species, each capable of displacing the species below it in the pecking order? These and many other questions are wide open for investigation.

7 Identification

δ : male
♀ : queen
☿ : worker

Fig. 26. Glossary diagram. The body of a bumblebee is divided into three obvious parts: the *head, thorax* and *abdomen*. The abdomen bears two sets of overlapping plates. The upper or *dorsal plates*, otherwise known as *tergites*, are referred to in the keys by the letter T (6 plates are visible in the female, and 7 in the male, numbered from the thorax end, T_{1-6} and T_{1-7} respectively). The lower or *ventral plates* are also known as *sternites*. The last few segments of the abdomen are loosely referred to as the *tail*, the tip of which houses the *sting* in the female and the *genital capsule* in the male. For the purposes of the keys three parts of the upper or dorsal surface of the thorax are distinguished: the *collar* at the front, the *scutellum* at the back and, in between, a band extending from one wing base to the other, the *interalar band*. The thorax bears the legs. In female *Bombus* the hind *tibia* is framed by long *corbicular hairs*, which form the *pollen basket* or *corbiculum*. The two *antennae* are divided into segments, which are numbered (as in Chart B, p. 55). The two *mandibles* work from side to side, and between them is the *tongue* or *proboscis*, which can be folded away underneath the head when the bee is not feeding.

Most areas of Britain harbour only a few bumblebee species and with practice these can be recognised on sight. In order to gain experience it is necessary to take a number of specimens through the main keys (pp. 57–69). These keys are not difficult to use, but if they look forbidding at first, start by making a guess at the name of your specimen using the colour plates (pp. 44–5) and the Quick-Check Key (p. 55). The Quick-Check Key deals only with workers and queens of the common species of true bumblebees, and uses only their most obvious features. It is therefore unreliable, but it may help give you a sense of direction before you work through the main keys. Terms used in the main keys are explained in the glossary diagram (fig. 26).

The main keys include all the species that have been recorded in Britain, and whenever possible they separate similarly coloured species on the basis of structural characters – which are less variable, and therefore more reliable, than hair colour. Throughout the keys *colour features refer to the coat of hairs* and not to the underlying cuticle (which is always black). Bear in mind that hair colour may fade during life. Many species produce dark-haired specimens. For British populations of some species these are too rare to be considered in the keys, but the dark forms are illustrated for those species in which they

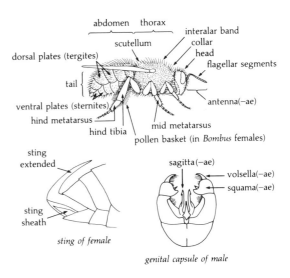

sting of female

genital capsule of male

Chart A. Is the specimen a true bumblebee (*Bombus*), or a cuckoo bumblebee (*Psithyrus*), or neither?

	Hoverflies, and other hairy flies	Other bees	True bumblebees (*Bombus*)	Cuckoo bumblebees (*Psithyrus*)
Antennae				
Wings: one pair or 2?	1 pair	2 pairs		
First submarginal cell divided from front to back by a pale narrow cross-bar? (thinner than veins in general)		No	Yes[a]	
Hairs on abdomen dense or sparse?			dense	sparse
Outer surface of hind tibia — female			shiny, flat and hairless; framed with long hairs	dull, convex and hairy; not framed with long hairs
Outer surface of hind tibia — male			shiny, flattish, with few (unbranched) hairs	dull, convex, with many (branched) hairs [b]
Tips of male genital capsule dark and horny, or pale and pliable?			dark	pale
Female mandibles square-ended or triangular-ended?			square-ended	triangular-ended

[a] Also present, but very faint, in *Anthophora* species
[b] Also applies to *B. pomorum*.

Chart B. Is the bumblebee a male or a female (queen or worker)?

	Male	Female
Antenna: 12 or 13 segments?	1 ... 13	1 ... 12
Abdominal segments visible from above: 6 or 7?	1 2 3 4 5 6 7	1 2 3 4 5 6
Tip of abdomen contains: a genital capsule or a sting (both shown extended)	genital capsule: top view — side view	sting: side view — top view — sting sheath

Quick-Check Key to queens and workers of the commonest species of true bumblebees (*Bombus*)

Before using this key, use Chart A and Chart B to ensure that your specimen is the queen or worker of a true bumblebee. Beware: this key does not include uncommon species, and cannot be used for critical identification. The species referred to below are illustrated on the cover.

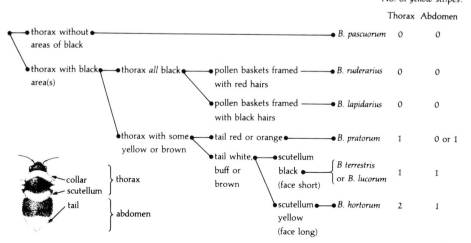

No. of *yellow* stripes:

	Thorax	Abdomen
B. pascuorum	0	0
B. ruderarius	0	0
B. lapidarius	0	0
B. pratorum	1	0 or 1
B terrestris or *B. lucorum*	1	1
B. hortorum	2	1

thorax without areas of black — *B. pascuorum*

thorax with black area(s) — thorax *all* black — pollen baskets framed with red hairs — *B. ruderarius*

pollen baskets framed with black hairs — *B. lapidarius*

thorax with some yellow or brown — tail red or orange — *B. pratorum*

tail white, buff or brown — scutellum black (face short) — B terrestris or *B. lucorum*

scutellum yellow (face long) — *B. hortorum*

collar — scutellum — } thorax

tail — } abdomen

occur quite frequently. In the plates, the male or worker of a species has been illustrated only if its colour markings differ appreciably from those of the queen. Bracketed statements in the main keys (other than instructions and special information) apply to additional information that is less easy to appreciate (for example, features that are best examined with a microscope), less reliable characters and characters whose states are inconsistent in the alternative lead and therefore not stated there.

First, is your specimen a bumblebee at all? The only other insects likely to be confused with bumblebees are solitary bees of the genus *Anthophora*, bee hawkmoths, and several hairy flies, including bee flies, warble flies, bot flies, bristle flies such as *Tachina grossa* (L.) and *Servillia* species, and hoverflies, some of which are very effective mimics (p. 30). Male *Anthophora* have yellow areas of cuticle (as opposed to hair) on the head; in bumblebees the cuticle is wholly black. Female *Anthophora* with black body hair differ from bumblebees most obviously in having a dense covering of stiff, orange hair on the outer surface of the hind tibia. Flies have only one pair of wings, whereas bees have two, but beware – bees zip their fore wings to their hind wings; a row of books on the hind wings catches on a ridge on the fore wing. In fresh specimens a pin can be used to disengage the bee's fore wing and hind wing, to prove that two pairs are present. Bees also differ from flies in the form of the antennae. Chart A show how to recognise a bumblebee, and how to distinguish true bumble bees from cuckoo bumblebees. Chart B deals with the distinction between males and females.

Note that hair colour varies geographically in some bumblebee species and for this reason features of coat colour used in the keys are not necessarily appropriate when identifying bumblebees from outside Britain and Eire.

In conjunction with the distribution maps (pp. 87–90, and ITE 1980) the keys can be used to check if one has a new distribution record for a species. Such records are a valuable addition to our knowledge and they can be registered (see p. 77).

O.E.P.-J. would be pleased to receive suggestions as to how the keys might be improved and made simpler to use. (*Correspondence address*: Bodhaulog, St Asaph, Clwyd, North Wales LL17 0LY.)

I.1

I.2

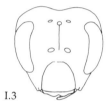

I.3

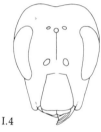

I.4

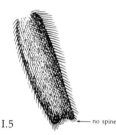

I.5 ←— no spine

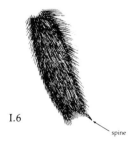

I.6

spine

I   Female true bumblebees (*Bombus*)

Note: Many structural characters are seen most easily in large females: in particular, sting sheath characters are most obvious and well developed in queens. To help confirm your identification after using this key compare the sting sheath with the illustrations in pl. 5. To view the sting sheath, extend the sting with forceps, turn the shaft upwards so that the tip points towards the bumblebee's head, then view the sting base from the bee's rear, end-on, using a binocular microscope (see Chart B, p. 55). The sting must be extended when the bee is still soft, soon after death; if the specimen has become rigid, relax it first (technique, p. 70). For definitions of terms used below, refer to the glossary diagram (fig. 26, p. 53).

1 Thorax all black (at most a few pale hairs at front and rear)   2

– Thorax not all black   7

2 Tail (T_4–T_6) red or orange red   3

– Tail black   ***B. ruderatus*** (pl. 1.9) and ***B. hortorum*** (dark forms)

Dark forms are frequent in *B. ruderatus* and rare in *B. hortorum*, and the two species cannot always be distinguished reliably. In *B. ruderatus* the coat is shorter and more even, and the very long face is relatively broad; queens are relatively large and sculpturing on T_6 is very marked (I.1). In *B. hortorum* the coat is longer and less even, and the very long face is relatively narrow; queens are somewhat smaller and sculpturing on T_6 is less marked (I.2). *B. ruderatus* is rare and local, and appears to have declined throughout much of its previous range in England. *B. hortorum* is common, widely distributed, and frequently found in gardens.

3 Face short, about as long as wide (as I.3)   4

– Face long, about $1\frac{1}{2}$ times as long as wide (as I.4); (hairs framing the pollen basket black, sometimes tipped by yellowish-red; T_1 and T_2 black; black on T_3 merging into red of tail)   ***B. pomorum*** (similar to *B. lapidarius*, pl. 2.1) Not found in Britain since 1864. All specimens from Deal on the Kent coast. Almost certainly a rare immigrant from the continent.

4 Pollen basket framed by black hairs; no spine at tip of mid metatarsus (I.5)   5

– Pollen basket framed by red hairs; mid metatarsus with spine at tip (I.6)   6

I.7

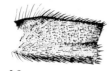

I.8

5 Outer surface of hind metatarsus densely covered with short yellowish-white hair (I.7; use a dissecting microscope); (inner projections of sting sheath simple (pl. 5.1))
      B. lapidarius (pl. 2.1)
   Common and widely distributed in Britain, except in Scotland. Predominantly a lowland species; often found in gardens.

– Outer surface of hind metatarsus shiny black with few hairs (I.8); (inner projections of sting sheath inwardly swollen (pl. 5.2))
      B. cullumanus (similar to *B. lapidarius*, pl. 2.1)
   Very rare. Associated with chalkland habitats in southern England. Unrecorded since 1926 and perhaps extinct in Britain.

6 Surface of 5th and 6th dorsal plates dull between the pits; (inner projections of sting sheath very broad, almost meeting in midline (pl. 5.3))   **B. ruderarius** (pl. 2.3)
   Locally common, particularly in south and east England, but appears to be getting rarer. Predominantly a lowland species; sometimes found in gardens.

– Surface of 5th and 6th dorsal plates shiny between the pits; (sting sheath as *B. ruderarius* (pl. 5.3))
      B. sylvarum (dark form)
   Only males of this continental colour form have been recorded in Britain, at Newhaven on the East Sussex coast.

7 Thorax buff, yellowish-brown or ginger all over, sometimes with black hairs mixed in, but without black areas (mid metatarsus with spine, as I.6)   8

– Thorax with black areas   10

8 Black hairs on upperside of abdomen present at least on sides of the 2nd, 3rd and 4th dorsal plates (i.e. T_2–T_4; if necessary use a lens); (inner projections of sting sheath narrow (pl. 5.4))   **B. pascuorum** (pl. 3.5, 3.6 and 3.7)
   Common throughout Britain. Frequently found in gardens.

– No black hairs on upperside of abdomen, except on T_6[*]
                                                             9

[*] *B. muscorum* subspecies *allenelus*, found on the Aran Islands, Eire, and some individuals of *B. muscorum* subspecies *liepeterseni*, from the Outer Hebridean Islands, have black on T_1 and the sides of T_2.

I.9

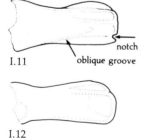

I.10

9 No black hairs on upperside of thorax; T_2 without a distinct brown band; (coat longer, more dense and of very even length, giving a velvety, crew-cut appearance; abdomen seen from above more rectangular (pl. 3.4); inner part of sting sheath undivided (pl. 5.5); hairs at sides of T_3 arise from little bumps (I.9: use a microscope))

B. muscorum (pl. 3.4)
Local and uncommon throughout the British Isles, especially in the south. Most frequent in damp or marshy inland and coastal sites, e.g. moorland, fens, salt marshes. Appears to have declined throughout much of its range in Britain in recent years.

– A few black hairs on upperside of thorax, especially above the wing bases (use a lens); T_2 with very characteristic brown band (pl. 3.8); (coat shorter, less dense and of less even length; abdomen seen from above more triangular (pl. 3.8); inner projections of sting sheath divided (pl. 5.6); hairs at sides of T_3 arise from pits (I.10))

B. humilis (pl. 3.8)
Local and uncommon. Restricted to southern England, particularly coastal and chalkland areas. Has become much less common in central England.

Sometimes it may be difficult to distinguish whether a specimen is *B. muscorum* or *B. humilis*.

10 Scutellum having black hair only 11

– Scutellum with at least some yellowish or brownish hairs 14

11 Tail orange-red (small species; yellow on 2nd dorsal plate (T_2) may be interrupted in the middle and is often absent in workers; inner projection of sting sheath simple (pl. 5.7))

B. pratorum (pl. 2.5)
Common throughout Britain. Frequently found in gardens.

– Tail white, buff or brown 12

12 Mandibles with notch and oblique groove, as in I.11 (use a dissecting microscope); (inner margin of sting sheath notched (as pl. 5.8)) 13

– Mandibles without notch or oblique groove (I.12); (small species; inner margin of sting sheath without notches (pl. 5.9))

B. soroeensis (pl. 3.1)
Local and rare. Found mainly in the north and west of Britain. Not recorded from Ireland. Has become much more scarce in central and southern England.

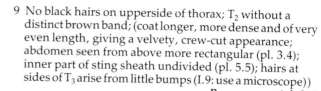

notch
oblique groove

I.11

I.12

I.13

I.14

13 Yellow stripes bright (lemon or creamy yellow); tail of queens and workers white or pinkish, without any trace of brownish at junction of black and white on T$_4$
B. lucorum (pl. 1.1) and **B. magnus**

These two species can be difficult to separate with confidence. *B. magnus* has a wider yellow collar, extending well below the level of the wing bases (I.13); the yellow band on T$_2$ is wider; and queens are often larger than those of *B. lucorum*. *B. magnus* is distributed in the north and west of Britain in exposed habitats such as heath and moorland. In contrast *B. lucorum* has a narrower yellow collar, ending level with, or just below the wing bases (I.14); the yellow on T$_2$ is narrower; and queens are often small relative to *B. magnus*. *B. lucorum* is common throughout Britain and is frequently found in gardens. The specific status of *B. magnus* requires further confirmation: it is, perhaps, a subspecies of *B. lucorum* adapted to a shorter season or differing climatic conditions.

– Yellowish stripes dark (brownish-yellow); queen tail buff or brownish, worker tail buff, or white with a thin brownish band next to the black of T$_4$
B. terrestris (pl. 1.3 and 1.4)

Common, particularly in the south of Britain. Not recorded from the north of Scotland. Frequently found in gardens.
Using the characters given above most females can be identified as *B. lucorum/B. magnus* or *B. terrestris*, but some workers are very difficult to distinguish, even for experts.

14 Tail red or orange*   15
– Tail white, brownish-yellow or greyish   16

15 Second and 3rd dorsal plates (T$_2$–T$_3$) reddish-orange, (T$_1$ black or yellow; T$_2$–T$_6$ reddish-orange, inclining to yellow at sides of T$_4$–T$_5$; abdominal hair long but even; yellow on rear of thorax C-shaped, being of similar width in the middle and at the sides; inner projections of sting sheath simple (as pl. 5.7))   **B. monticola** (pl. 2.8)
Quite common on upland moors, particularly where *Vaccinium* species grow. Recently recorded from one site in Ireland.

– Second dorsal plate (T$_2$) largely pale greenish-grey, with traces of black, at least on the sides; T$_3$ black, edged with pale greenish hairs; (T$_1$ pale greenish-grey; T$_4$–T$_6$ orange, edged with narrow band of greenish-white; coat rather thin and uneven; yellow on rear of thorax wider in the middle than at the sides; inner projections of sting sheath as in pl. 5.3)   **B. sylvarum** (pl. 2.7)
Local and uncommon lowland species. More frequent in southern England. Rare in Ireland.

* On the islands of the Outer Hebrides and Shetland *B. jonellus* (couplet 16) occurs in an orange-tailed form, rather than the usual white-tailed (mainland) form (pl. 1.6).

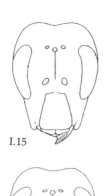

I.15

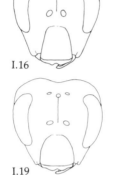

I.16

I.19

I.17   oblique groove

I.20   notch

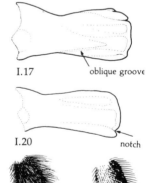

I.18   spine

16 Face long or medium length as in I.15 or I.16; mandibles with oblique groove but without notch (I.17; use a dissecting microscope); mid metatarsus with spine (as I.18; use a dissecting microscope or strong lens)   17

– Face short as in I.19; mandibles without oblique groove but with notch (I.20); mid metatarsus without spine (as I.21); (small species; inner projections of sting sheath simple (pl. 5.10))   ***B. jonellus*** (pl. 1.6)
Not uncommon, but quite local. Found throughout much of Britain, especially in areas of heath and moorland.

17 Sixth ventral plate without keel; (face long (as I.15); inner projections of sting sheath with characteristic notches (as pl. 5.11))
B. hortorum (pl. 1.5) and ***B. ruderatus*** (pl. 1.8 and 1.10)
In some cases, particularly small workers, it may not be possible to distinguish whether a specimen is *B. hortorum* or *B. ruderatus*. Typically, in *B. hortorum* the yellow of thorax and abdomen is bright; the rear thoracic band is C-shaped (that is, of about equal width along its length) and noticeably narrower in the middle than the collar (pl. 1.5); sculpturing on the 6th dorsal plate (T_6) is shallow (I.22); the coat is long and uneven; and T_1 and the base of T_2 are usually yellow. Queens are normally smaller than those of *B. ruderatus*.
In *B. ruderatus*, workers are usually undarkened or completely black (the latter are dealt with in couplet 2, p. 57), whereas in queens intermediate forms, showing variable degrees of darkening, are also frequent (pl. 1.10). In undarkened specimens the yellow of the thorax and abdomen is golden or brownish-yellow, the rear thoracic band is wider in the middle than at the sides and, at its middle, about as wide as the yellow collar (pl. 1.8); sculpturing on T_6 (which is best developed in queens) is deep (I.23); the coat is short and even; and on the abdomen yellow is usually restricted to T_1 and often replaced in the middle by black. Queens are usually larger than those of *B. hortorum*. In darkened specimens of both *B. hortorum* and *B. ruderatus* the tail may be grey or brownish (as in pl. 1.10), the relative width of the thoracic bands is variable, and one or both of the bands may be absent. For information on distributions and abundance see couplet 2, p. 57.

– Sixth ventral plate with pronounced keel, or ridge, along the middle, as in I.24; (face medium length (as I.16); inner projections of sting sheath without notches (as pl. 5.12))   18

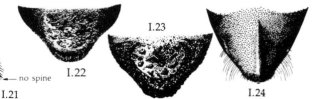

I.23

I.22

no spine

I.21

I.24

18 Abdomen brownish-yellow all over; (thorax brownish-
yellow with a black or dark grey band between the wings;
coat long)   ***B. distinguendus*** (pl. 3.3)
Rare; very local. Most frequent in north and west Scotland. Has
become much scarcer throughout England.

– First three dorsal plates (T_1–T_3) of abdomen black, often
with a narrow fringe of brownish or pale hairs at the rear
edge of each; T_4–T_5 whitish; (coat very short, especially on
front segments of abdomen)   ***B. subterraneus*** (pl. 3.9)
Rare; very local. Restricted to the south of England. Has declined
greatly in recent years.

II.1

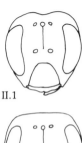

II.2

II   Male true bumblebees (*Bombus*)

Note: To help confirm your identification after using this
key, compare the genital capsule with the illustrations in
pl. 6. The genital capsule should be extended gently with
forceps while the bee is still soft, soon after death. If the
bee has become rigid, relax it first (technique, p. 70). If the
genitalia do not correspond with those of the species
name reached via the key, then reject the key identification in favour of the best match in pl. 6 and go through
the key again to see what went wrong. For information on
species distributions and abundance see relevant couplets (referred to below) in key I. For definitions of terms
used below, refer to the glossary diagram (fig. 26, p. 53).

1 Thorax entirely black, or at most with scattered brownish-
yellow hairs at front and rear   2

– Thorax with yellow, whitish, buff or ginger areas, at least
at front   4

2 Face short, about as long as wide (as II.1)   3

– Face long, about 1¼ times as long as wide (as II.2); (genital
capsule as pl. 6.1)
B. hortorum and ***B. ruderatus*** (dark forms; similar to ♀,
pl. 1.9)
See couplet 2, p. 57, for distribution and abundance. Dark forms
occur frequently in *B. ruderatus* and infrequently in *B. hortorum*,
and the species are not easy to distinguish: colour of the beard on
the mandibles may be useful (black in *B. hortorum*, reddish in
B. ruderatus), as well as the length and position of hairs on the rear
edge of the hind tibia (continued round the end, and longer at the
base in *B. hortorum* (II.3), stopping short of the end, and shorter at
the base in *B. ruderatus* (II.4)).

II.3

II.4

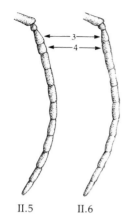

II.5   II.6

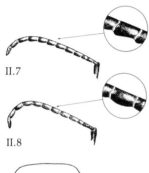

II.7

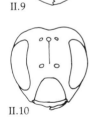

II.8

II.9

II.10

3 Third antennal segment much longer than 4th (II.5); (genital capsule pl. 6.2)   *B. ruderarius* (pl. 2.4)
See couplet 6, p. 58, for information on distribution and abundance.

– Third antennal segment only a little longer than 4th (II.6); (genital capsule pl. 6.3)
B. sylvarum (dark form; similar to pl. 2.4)
Males of this continental form have been recorded, on one occasion, from Newhaven, East Sussex.

4 Thorax buff, brown or ginger all over, sometimes with black hairs mixed in, but without black areas   5

– Thorax with black areas   7

5 Upperside of abdomen with at least some black hairs among the brownish ones (use a lens); mid antennal segments swollen underneath, more so at their apical ends (II.7); (genital capsule pl. 6.4)
B. pascuorum (similar to ♀ and ♀̵, pl. 3.5, 3.6 and 3.7)
Common throughout Britain. Frequently found in gardens.

– Upperside of abdomen without any black hairs among the brownish ones;* mid antennal segments less swollen underneath, swellings symmetrical (II.8)   6

6 Thorax with at least a few black hairs, especially above the wing bases (use a lens); (brownish band on T$_2$; coat shorter, uneven and less dense; genital capsule pl. 6.5)
B. humilis (similar to ♀, pl. 3.8)
See couplet 9, p. 59, for information on distribution and abundance.

– Thorax without any black hairs; (coat longer, more even; genital capsule pl. 6.6)
B. muscorum (similar to ♀, pl. 3.4)
See couplet 9, p. 59, for information on distribution and abundance.

7 Face long, about 1¼ times as long as wide (as II.9)   8

– Face short, about as long as wide (as II.10)   10

8 Tail white or grey-brown; (genital capsule pl. 6.1)   9

– Tail red; (mandibles without a beard; genital capsule pl. 6.7)   *B. pomorum* (similar to *P. rupestris* ♂, pl. 4.2)
For information on previous records see couplet 3, p. 57.

* *B. muscorum* subspecies *allenelus*, which is found on the Aran Islands, Eire, and some individuals of *B. muscorum* subspecies *liepeterseni*, from the Outer Hebridean Islands, have black hair on T$_1$ and T$_2$.

II.11

II.12

9 Yellow front and rear bands on thorax broad, sharply separated from black, and equally broad in midline; coat shorter and more even; (mandibles with reddish beard; hairs on rear edge of hind tibia stopping short of its tip, and shorter at its base (II.11) than in *B. hortorum* (II.12))

B. ruderatus (similar to ♀, pl. 1.8 and 1.10) Banded and dark forms frequent. Dark forms sometimes with grey-brown tail. Intermediate forms rare. See couplet 2, p. 57, for information on distribution and abundance.

– Yellow front and rear bands on thorax often narrow, less sharply separated from black; rear band narrower than the front one; coat longer and less even; (mandibles with blackish beard; hairs on rear edge of hind tibia continuing round its tip, and longer at its base (II.12) than in *B. ruderatus* (II.11))

B. hortorum (similar to ♀, pl. 1.5) Banded forms common, dark forms (see couplet 2, p. 57) infrequent. Intermediate forms occur, with variable degrees of darkening of yellow bands and white tail. See couplet 2, p. 57, for information on distribution and abundance.

In some cases it may not be possible to distinguish whether a specimen is *B. hortorum* or *B. ruderatus*.

10 Front and rear bands on thorax of roughly equal width in midline   11

– Rear band absent or much narrower in the middle than the front band   17

11 Tail reddish or orange, at least on T_6 12

– Tail white or a greenish- or yellowish-brown   15

12 Genital capsule (refer to fig. 26 for explanation of terms): tips of volsellae sharply pointed, tips of sagittae pointing slightly outwards (as pl. 6.2 and 6.3)   13

– Tips of volsellae blunt, tips of sagittae pointing inwards and hook-like (pl. 6.8 and 6.9)   14

13 Third antennal segment much longer than 4th (II.13); (genital capsule pl. 6.2)
B. ruderarius (similar to ♂ *B. lapidarius* (pl. 2.2) but with less yellow hair)
See couplet 6, p. 58, for information on distribution and abundance.

– Third antennal segment only a little longer than 4th (II.14); (genital capsule pl. 6.3)
B. sylvarum (similar to ♀, pl. 2.7)
See couplet 15, p. 60, for information on distribution and abundance.

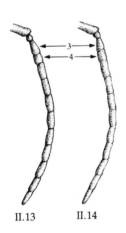

II.13   II.14

14 Volsellae extending well beyond tips of sagittae (pl. 6.8); tips of volsellae elongated, and flattened on their inner surfaces (pl. 6.8); (flagellar segments of antennae somewhat curved in profile)

B. cullumanus (similar to ♂ *B. pratorum*, pl. 2.6) Very rare. Associated with chalkland habitats in southern England. Unrecorded since 1926 and perhaps extinct in Britain.

– Volsellae extending only just beyond tips of sagittae (pl. 6.9); tips of volsellae not elongated or flattened on their inner surfaces (pl. 6.9); (flagellar segments almost straight-sided)

B. jonellus (as pl. 1.7, but with an orange tail) This colour form of *B. jonellus* occurs on the Outer Hebridean Islands and on the Shetlands.

15 Abdomen with at least some black hairs, which may be restricted to the sides of T_2 16

– Abdomen without any black hairs; (thoracic bands and abdomen brownish-yellow; facial hairs mainly pale; genital capsule pl. 6.10)

B. distinguendus (similar to ♀, pl. 3.3) See couplet 18, p. 62, for information on distribution and abundance.

16 Abdomen largely greenish-yellow; (hair fringe on hind tibia at most equal to tibial width; body hair short; abdomen elongate; facial hairs mainly dark; genital capsule as pl. 6.10)   *B. subterraneus* (pl. 3.10) See couplet 18, p. 62, for information on distribution and abundance.

– T_3 and T_4 black, tail white or yellowish; (hair fringe on hind tibia much longer than tibial width; body hair long; abdomen rounded; facial hairs mainly pale; thoracic bands, T_1 and base of T_2 yellow; genital capsule pl. 6.9)   *B. jonellus* (pl. 1.7) See couplet 16, p. 61, for information on distribution and abundance.

17 Tail white or buff-brown   18

– Tail orange or reddish   20

18 Hind metatarsus with slender base and long hair fringe on rear edge (II.15); 3rd antennal segment shorter than 5th (II.16); (hair long; genital capsule pl. 6.11)   *B. soroeensis* (pl. 3.2) See couplet 12, p. 59, for information on distribution and abundance.

– Hind metatarsus with broad base and short hair fringe on rear edge (II.17); 3rd and 5th antennal segments of about equal length (as II.18); (hair short; genital capsule as pl. 6.12)   19

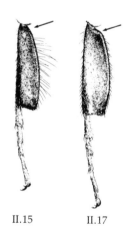

II.15   II.17

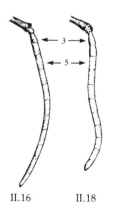

II.16   II.18

19 Tail pure white; yellow of thorax and T$_2$ pale lemon or
    creamy yellow; coat long and uneven; facial hair yellow,
    black or a mixture of the two; yellow hair may be present
    on the rear of the thorax
                                    B. lucorum (pl. 1.2) and *B. magnus*
    So far males of these two species cannot be distinguished mor-
    phologically; characters that will allow us to separate them need
    to be identified. For information on distribution and abundance
    see couplet 13, p. 60.

–   Tail off-white or buff-brown; yellow of thorax and T$_2$ dark
    golden or brownish-yellow; coat short and even; facial
    hair black; no yellow hair on the rear of the thorax
                                    B. terrestris (similar to ♀, pl. 1.3)
    For information on distribution and abundance, see couplet 13,
    p. 60.
    Using the characters given above most males can be distin-
    guished as *B. lucorum/B. magnus* or *B. terrestris*, but some speci-
    mens are very difficult to identify, even for experts.

20 Hair on 2nd and 3rd dorsal plates (T$_2$ and T$_3$) black or
    yellow   21

–   Hair on T$_2$ and T$_3$ red; (genital capsule as pl. 6.13)
                                    B. monticola (similar to ♀, pl. 2.8)
    For information on distribution and abundance see couplet 15, p.
    60.

21 Genital capsule (refer to fig. 26 for explanation of terms)
    with hooked end to sagitta (pl. 6.13); (hair long and
    uneven; hair on T$_1$ and T$_2$ yellow (may be reduced or
    rarely absent); T$_3$ black; T$_4$ black or orange; remainder of
    abdomen orange)   *B. pratorum* (pl. 2.6)
    Common throughout Britain. Frequently found in gardens.

–   Genital capsule (refer to fig. 26 for explanation of terms)
    with spiky end to sagitta (pl. 6.14); (hair short and even;
    hair on T$_1$ black (at most a trace of yellow); T$_2$ and T$_3$ black;
    remainder of abdomen red)   *B. lapidarius* (pl. 2.2)
    For information on distribution and abundance see couplet 5,
    p. 58.

III   Female cuckoo bumblebees (*Psithyrus*)

Note: In all cases confirm your identification by comparing the two bulges or ridges (callosities) on the last (6th) ventral plate with the illustrations in pl. 7. For definition of terms used below, refer to the glossary diagram (fig. 26, p. 53).

1 Tail (T$_4$–T$_6$) entirely red; thorax and rest of abdomen black; bulges (callosities) on 6th ventral plate very large, fin-like (pl. 7.1) and visible from above; wings dark smoky-brown   ***P. rupestris*** (pl. 4.1)
Takes over nests of *B. lapidarius*. Rare, but less so in the south and east. Not recorded from Scotland. Has declined greatly during this century.

– Tail not entirely red; callosities on 6th ventral plate smaller (pl. 7.2–6) than those of *P. rupestris* (pl. 7.1)   2

2 Callosities on 6th ventral plate very small and inconspicuous (pl. 7.2); (tip of abdomen strongly curved under; T$_3$–T$_4$ mainly white or yellowish-white)
P. sylvestris (pl. 4.3)
Takes over nests of *B. pratorum*, and sometimes *B. jonellus*. Widely distributed and locally common.

– Callosities on 6th ventral plate large and conspicuous (pl. 7.3–6)   3

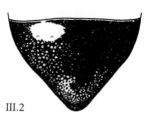

III.1

3 Callosities form a shallow U-shape (pl. 7.4); last dorsal plate (T$_6$) dull and closely pitted, with a distinct keel along the middle (III.1)   ***P. barbutellus*** (pl. 4.9)
Takes over nests of *B. hortorum*. Quite common; distributed throughout Britain.

– Callosities form a V-shape (pl. 7.3, 7.5 and 7.6); last dorsal plate (T$_6$) shiny   4

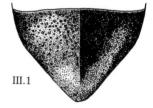

III.2

4 Tail without white hairs; (T$_6$ as III.2; 6th ventral plate pl. 7.3)   ***P. campestris*** (pl. 4.10)
Takes over nests of *B. pascuorum*, and possibly *B. humilis*. Darkened specimens are common; completely black specimens are rare. Quite common and widely distributed.

– Tail with white hairs   5

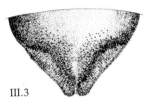

III.3

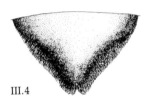

III.4

5 Callosities end short of the tip of 6th ventral plate (pl. 7.5); T_6 not shiny (III.3); (yellow of thorax and abdomen darker; larger bee with shorter coat; T_3 lemon-yellow at the sides; scutellum (rear part of the thorax) black)

P. vestalis (pl. 4.7)

Takes over nests of *B. terrestris*. Common in the southern half of Britain. Not recorded from Scotland or Ireland.

– Callosities end near tip of 6th ventral plate (pl. 7.6); T_6 shiny (III.4); (yellow of thorax and abdomen paler (and rapidly fading); usually smaller bee, with longer shaggy coat; T_3 pale yellow at the sides; scutellum often has pale hairs)   *P. bohemicus* (pl. 4.5)

Takes over nests of *B. lucorum*, and possibly also *B. magnus*. Common, particularly in northern and western Britain.

IV   Male cuckoo bumblebees (*Psithyrus*)

Note: To help confirm your identification after using this key, compare the genital capsule with the illustrations in pl. 8. The genital capsule should be extended gently with forceps while the bee is still soft, soon after death. If the bee has become rigid, relax it first (technique, p. 70). If the genitalia do not correspond with those of the species name reached via the key, then reject the key identification in favour of the best match in pl. 8 and try the key again to see what went wrong. For information on species distributions and abundance see relevant couplets (referred to below) in key III. For definitions of terms used below, refer to the glossary diagram (fig. 26, p. 53).

IV.1

1 Last ventral plate bearing a black hair-tuft on each side (IV.1); (genital capsule pl. 8.1)

P. campestris (pl. 4.11 and 4.12)

Entirely black specimens are quite common. For information on distribution, abundance and host species see couplet 4, p. 67.

– Last ventral plate without these tufts (as IV.2)   2

IV.2

2 Tail mainly red or red-brown; (genital capsule pl. 8.2)

P. rupestris (pl. 4.2)

For information on distribution, abundance and host species see couplet 1, p. 67.

– Tail mainly yellow or white   3

3 Seventh dorsal plate (tip of tail seen from above) usually red-haired (occasionally yellow-haired; genital capsule pl. 8.3)   *P. sylvestris* (pl. 4.4)

For information on distribution, abundance and host species see couplet 2, p. 67.

– Seventh dorsal plate black-haired   4

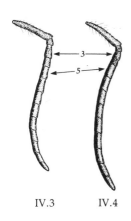

IV.3   IV.4

4 Third and 5th segments of antenna about equal in length
(IV.3); (T$_3$ with yellow to whitish patch on each side, black
in the middle; genital capsule pl. 8.4)
                                    P. bohemicus (pl. 4.6)
For information on distribution, abundance and host species see
couplet 5, p. 68.

− Third segment of antenna obviously shorter than 5th (as
IV.4)   5

5 Last ventral plate with a small mound on each side of
midline, near the tip (IV.2); (T$_3$ without obvious *patches* of
white or yellow on each side; genital capsule pl. 8.5)
                            P. barbutellus (similar to ♀, pl. 4.9)
For information on distribution, abundance and host species see
couplet 3, p. 67.

− Last ventral plate without a small mound on each side of
midline, near the tip (IV.1); (T$_3$ yellow (fading to white) at
the sides, usually black in the middle, but sometimes
yellow; genital capsule pl. 8.6)   *P. vestalis* (pl. 4.8)
For information on distribution, abundance and host species see
couplet 5, p. 68.

8 Techniques and approaches to original work

Catching and handling bumblebees for identification

It is usually quite easy to catch a bumblebee, either by placing a specimen tube over it while it is perched on a flower, or by sweeping it up with a butterfly net. A collapsible pocket net is convenient and can be purchased from Watkins and Doncaster (address, p. 71). To transfer the specimen to a tube, hold the net bag up by its tip – which will encourage the bumblebee to move upwards – then carefully slide the tube up inside.

Ethyl acetate or chloroform may be used for killing bees; ethyl acetate is preferable because it leaves the bee relaxed. Apply the killing fluid to 1 centimetre depth of plaster of Paris previously set into the base of a jar or tube. To prevent the specimen from getting damp, keep the plaster and container dry and use just a few drops of killing fluid. Leave the bumblebee in the killing jar for at least half an hour to make sure it is dead.

Mount the bee on an entomological pin passed through the centre of the thorax. If you want to position the body parts (as in the plates) press the pin into a sheet of cork or polyethylene foam (see p. 71). The bee's wings can be held forward by a pin positioned between the bases of the fore and hind wings, on each side. Each hind wing has a row of small hooks on the leading edge; these can be attached to a ridge on the back of the fore wing (as in life) to keep the hind wing in position. Claws on the tips of the legs will grip the surface to which the bee is pinned, and can be used to keep the legs in position. Before setting the bee, it may be desirable to extend the sting or genital capsule with forceps, to enable it to be examined later on. After several days the body parts will remain rigidly set in position.

Sometimes it may be necessary to relax and reset a bumblebee. This can be done by placing the specimen in a small airtight container in which there is a dish of water. After 2–3 days in this high humidity the membranes become soft and pliable, and with care the bee can then be reset. Do not leave the specimen at high humidity for too long, or it will go mouldy.

Every specimen must have a label attached to its pin indicating when, where and by whom it was caught. A second label bearing the species name of the bee may be placed below the first. When identifying a specimen always use the best light source available. Vary the angle of observation: this can be done easily if the bumblebee is

Behaviour, 9, 164–201.
Michener, C. D. (1974). *The Social Behaviour of the Bees: A Comparative Study.* Cambridge, Mass.: Harvard University Press.

Moore, P. D. & Webb, J. A. (1978). *An Illustrated Guide to Pollen Analysis.* London: Hodder & Stoughton.

Nair, M. K. & Narasimhan, R. (1963). Acidified safranin-aniline blue: a selective stain for pollen tubes in sugar cane. *Stain Technology,* 38, 341–2.

Newsholme, E. A., Crabtree, B., Higgins, S. J., Thornton, S. D. & Start, C. (1972). The activities of fructose diphosphatase in flight muscles from the bumble-bee and the role of this enzyme in heat generation. *Biochemical Journal,* 128, 89–97.

Palm, N.-B. (1948). Normal and pathological histology of the ovaries in *Bombus* Latr. (Hymenoptera). *Opuscula Entomologica Supplementum,* 7, 1–101.

Parker, R. E. (1979). *Introductory Statistics for Biology.* Studies in Biology no. 43. London: Edward Arnold.

*Plath,O. E. (1934). *Bumblebees and their Ways.* New York: Macmillan.

Plowright, R. C. & Jay, S. C. (1966). Rearing bumble bee colonies in captivity. *Journal of Apicultural Research,* 5(3), 155–65.

Poinar, Jr, G. O. & van der Laan, P. A. (1972). Morphology and life history of *Sphaerularia bombi* (Dufour) (Nematodea). *Nematologica,* 18, 239–52.

Pomeroy, N. & Plowright, R. C. (1980). Maintenance of bumble bee colonies in observation hives (Hymenoptera: Apidae). *Canadian Entomologist,* 112, 321–6.

Prŷs-Jones, O. E. (1982). Ecological studies of foraging and life history in bumblebees.

PhD Thesis, University of Cambridge.

Prŷs-Jones, O. E. (1986). Foraging behaviour and the activity of substrate cycle enzymes in bumblebees. *Animal Behaviour,* 34, 609–11.

Prŷs-Jones, O. E. & Crabtree, B. (1983). Measurements of the activity of substrate cycle enzymes in bumblebees. Unpublished.

Prŷs-Jones, O. E., Ólafsson, E. & Kristjánsson, K. (1981). The Icelandic bumblebee fauna and its distributional ecology. *Journal of Apicultural Research,* 20(3), 189–97.

Richards, K. W. (1973). Biology of *Bombus polaris* Curtis and *B. hyperboreus* Schönherr at Lake Hazen, Northwest Territories (Hymenoptera: Bombini). *Quaestiones Entomologicae,* 9, 115–57.

Richards, O. W. (1927). The specific characters of the British humblebees (Hymenoptera). *Transactions of the Entomological Society of London,* 75, 233–68.

Sawyer, R. (1981). *Pollen Identification for Beekeepers,* ed. R. S. Pickard. Cardiff: University College Cardiff Press. (Available from IBRA see IBRA (1975) above for address.)

Sladen, F. W. L. (1989). *The Humble-bee, its Life History and how to Domesticate it.* Including *The Humble Bee* (1892). Logaston Press.

Smith, K. G. V. (1969). Diptera; Conopidae. *Handbooks for the Identification of British Insects,* X(3a). London: Royal Entomological Society of London.

Svensson, B. G. (1979). Patrolling behaviour of bumble bee males (Hymenoptera, Apidae) in a subalpine/alpine area, Swedish Lapland. *Zoon,* 7, 67–94.

Synge, A. D. (1947). Pollen

collection by honeybees (*Apis mellifera*). *Journal of Animal Ecology,* 16, 122–38.

Unwin, D. M. (1978). Simple techniques for microclimate measurement. *Journal of Biological Education,* 12, 179–89.

Unwin, D. M. (1980). *Microclimate Measurement for Ecologists.* New York & London: Academic Press.

Unwin, D. M. & Corbet, S. A. (1991). *Insects, plants and microclimate.* Naturalists' Handbooks No. 15. Slough: The Richmond Publishing Co. Ltd.

WATCH (1987). *Really Useful Insects Project Pack.* Slough: The Richmond Publishing Co. Ltd.

Weast, R. C. (1978). *CRC Handbook of Chemistry and Physics,* p. D-308. Florida: CRC Press Inc.

Williams, P. H. (1982). The distribution and decline of British bumble bees (*Bombus* Latr.). *Journal of Apicultural Research,* 21(4), 236–45.

Williams, P. H. (1989). Why are there so many species of bumble bees at Dungeness? *Botanical Journal of the Linnean Society,* 101, 31–44.

Willmer, P. G. (1983). Thermal constraints on activity patterns in nectar-feeding insects. *Ecological Entomology,* 8, 455–69.

Yalden, P. E. (1982). Pollen collected by the bumblebee *Bombus monticola* Smith in the Peak District, England. *Journal of Natural History,* 16, 823–32.

Yarrow, I. H. H. (1970). Is *Bombus inexspectatus* (Thalcu) a worker-less obligate parasite? (Hym., Apidae). *Insectes Sociaux,* 17, 95–112.

Yeo, P. F. & Corbet, S. A. (1983). *Solitary Wasps.* Naturalists' Handbooks no. 3. Cambridge: CUP, now from The Richmond Publishing Co. Ltd.

Synonymy

A summary of specific names for British bumblebees, and some works in which they appear. Presently used names are given in bold type. The list only includes those species whose names have changed this century.

Sladen (1912)	Richards (1927)	Yarrow, in Free & Butler (1959)	Alford (1975) and ITE (1980)	Fitton & others (1978)	Name used in this work	Name changes suggested by Day (1979)[a]
Bombus:						
latreillellus →	**subterraneus** ··········				······→	
derhamellus →	**ruderarius** ··········				······→	
muscorum ·················		→ { muscorum / smithianus }	→ *muscorum* ······		······→	→ laevis
helferanus →	solstitialis ·······	→ **humilis** ········			············→	→ muscorum
agrorum ·········			→ **pascuorum** ··········		······→	
soroënsis ·····?·······			→ **soroeensis** ·······		······→	
lucorum ········			→ { lucorum / magnus }	········· → lucorum ·····	→ { lucorum / magnus } ··	·····→ terrestris
terrestris ········					············	→ audax
lapponicus ··········				→ **monticola** ·······	······→	
Psithyrus:						
distinctus ······→	**bohemicus** ··········				······→	

[a] Day, sorting out errors arising from earlier authors' misidentifications of type specimens, pointed out that strict observance of the international rules of zoological nomenclature would require these changes. The rules can be formally waived in special cases, and this may prove to be such a case: some of the proposed names are already in use for other similar species, and the changes would cause considerable confusion. Until it is clear whether the new names will be adopted, we retain the names used in other publications to which readers are likely to refer. Meanwhile, authors will need to take particular care to state whether or not they are following Day's usage.

Index

Page numbers in bold type indicate species in identification keys.

anaesthetics, 71
antennae, 53, 54, 55

Bees, Wasps and Ants Recording
    Scheme (BWARS), 77
body temperature control, 14
    energetic costs, 35, 37
    enzyme activity, 36
    muscular activity, 35–6
body weight determination, 73
Bombus (true bumblebees)
    annual cycle, 12–21
    behaviour like Psithyrus, 28
    distribution, 2–4; records of, 77
    identification: females, 55,
        57–62; males, 55, 62–6
    and mimic species, 4, 28, 30–1,
        54, 56
    number of species, 2
    simple and complex species,
        15–16
Bombus agrorum, 82
Bombus audax, 82
Bombus cullumanus, 2, 58, 65
    genital capsule, 46
    sting sheath, 45
Bombus derhamellus, 82
Bombus distinguendus, 2, 62, 65
    genital capsule, 46
    sting sheath, 45
Bombus helferanus, 82
Bombus hortorum, 6, 7, 20, 55, 57,
    61, 62, 64
    distribution, 2, 3
    flight levels, 19
    flower-visiting patterns, 42, 43
    genital capsule, 45
    mating scars, 72
    natural history, 8–10
    seasonal flight activity, 9
    tongue length and foraging
        behaviour, 8, 10
Bombus humilis, 59, 63, 82
    distribution, 2, 3
    genital capsule, 46
    sting sheath, 45
Bombus jonellus, 60n, 61, 65
    distribution, 2, 3
    genital capsule, 46
    male marking substances, 18
    sting sheath, 45

Bombus laevis, 82
Bombus lapidarius, 6, 7, 55, 58, 66
    distribution, 2, 3
    flight levels, 19
    flower-visiting patterns, 43
    genital capsule, 46
    male marking substances, 18
    sting sheath, 45
Bombus lapponicus, 82
Bombus latreillellus, 82
Bombus lucorum, 6, 7, 55, 60, 66, 82
    distribution, 2, 3
    flight levels, 19
    flower-visiting patterns, 43
    male marking substances, 18
    sting sheath, 45
Bombus magnus, 2, 60, 66, 82
Bombus monticola, 44, 60, 66, 82
    distribution, 2, 3
    male marking substances, 18
Bombus muscorum, 59, 63, 82
    distribution, 2, 3
    genital capsule, 46
    sting sheath, 45
Bombus muscorum subsp.
    allenelus, 58n, 63n
Bombus muscorum subsp.
    liepeterseni, 58n, 63n
Bombus pascuorum, 6, 7, 55, 58, 82
    distribution, 2, 3
    flight levels, 19
    flower-visiting patterns, 43
    genital capsule, 46
    life cycle, and latitude, 21
    male marking substances, 18
    natural history, 10–11
    seasonal flight activity, 9
    sting sheath, 45
    tongue length and foraging
        behaviour, 10–11, 41
Bombus pomorum, 2, 57, 63
    genital capsule, 46
Bombus pratorum, 6, 7, 19, 55, 59,
    66
    distribution, 2, 3
    flight levels, 19
    flower-visiting patterns, 42, 43
    genital capsule, 46
    male marking substances, 18
    natural history, 11
    seasonal flight activity, 9

Bombus pratorum (continued)
  sting sheath, 45
  tongue length and foraging
    behaviour, 10, 11, 41
Bombus ruderarius, 6, **55**, **58**, **63**, **64**,
  82
  distribution, 2, 3
  sting sheath, 45
Bombus ruderatus, **57**, **61**, **62**, **64**
  distribution, 2, 3
  genital capsule, 46
  sting sheath, 45
Bombus smithianus, 82
Bombus solstitialis, 82
Bombus soroeensis, **59**, **65**, 82
Bombus soroënsis, 82
  distribution, 2, 3
  genital capsule, 46
  male marking substances, 18
  sting sheath, 45
Bombus subterraneus, 2, 3, **62**, **65**,
  82
Bombus sylvarum, **58**, **60**, **63**, **64**
  distribution, 2, 3
  flight levels, 19
  genital capsule, 46
Bombus terrestris, 6, 7, **55**, **60**, 82
  distribution, 2, 3
  flight levels, 19
  flower-visiting patterns, 43
  genital capsule, 46
  honeystomach, 40
  male marking substances, 18
  natural history, 6–8
  queen behaviour, 13–14
  seasonal flight activity, 9
  tongue length and foraging
    behaviour, 6, 41
Brachycoma devia, 31
Bumblebee Distribution Maps
  Scheme (BDMS), 77

carder bees, 10
colouration
  changes in, 6
  identification, 4, 53, 56
  see also mimicry
conopid flies, 31–2
cuckoo bumblebees, *see Psithyrus*

dissection, 72–3
distribution, 2–4
  records of, 77

eggs, 73
  hatching, 14
  laying and brooding, 14
  unfertilised, 16
entomological societies, 78

fat body, 13, 72

feeding of larvae, 14, 15
  pocket-makers, 7, 15
  pollen-storers, 7, 15
  and sex determination, 16
  and size of adults, 15
  see also foraging
females, 1
  identification: *Bombus*, 55,
    56–62; *Psithyrus*, 67–8
  Psithyrus, 28–9
  see also queens; workers
flight activity
  seasonal cycles, 9
flight levels, 17, 19
flower growing for bumblebees,
  24, 76–7
foraging, 14–15
  body temperature control, 35–6
  colour and scent of flowers, 42
  energetic costs, 35, 37
  energetic reward per flower,
    39–40
  flower selection, 39–40
  flower-visiting patterns, 41–2,
    42–3
  and fructose bisphosphatase
    activity, 36
  further investigations, 51–2
  learning, 41
  optimal foraging theory, 35
  pollen collection, 12, 14, 42–4
  see also nectar foraging
foraging seasons, 20–1
fructose bisphosphatase
  heat control and foraging
    behaviour, 36

genital capsules, 53, 55
  Bombus, 46, 54
  Psithyrus, 48, 54
grooming, 42, 43, 44

honeybees, 12
honeystomach, 18
  contents sampling, 71
  load estimation, 40
  removal of, 40, 72

identification, 53ff
  Bombus, 55; females, 55, 57–62;
    males, 55, 62–6; catching and
    handling bumblebees, 70–1
  and mimic species, 4, 28,
    30–1, 54, 56
  Psithyrus: females, 67–8;
    males, 68–9
inquilines, 4, 28

killing and mounting, 70–1

larval development, 14

see also feeding of larvae
life cycle lengths
 and latitude, 20
 short cycle species, 10, 20
life histories
 Bombus, 7, 12–21
 Psithyrus, 28–9

male marking substances, 17, 18
males, 1, 17
 identification: *Bombus*, 55, 62–6;
  Psithyrus, 68–9
 production of, 15, 16–17, 19
 reproductive behaviour, 17
 seasonal flight activity, 9
mandibles, 53, 54
marking bumblebees, 71
mating behaviour, 12, 16, 17
mating scars, 72
microclimate recording, 77
mimicry, 34, 56
 by hoverflies, 30–1, 54
 by *Psithyrus*, 4, 28, 54
mites, 32–3
Müllerian mimicry, 4, 28, 31, 34

names and synonyms, 5, 82
nectar
 concentration measurement,
  73–4
 energy content calculation, 74
 flower source evaluation, 49–50
nectar foraging, 38–43
 energetic reward per flower,
  39–40
 hole-biting in corolla tube, 6–8
 learning, 41
 water balance, 39
 see also honeystomach
nematode parasite, 32–4
nest associates, 30–2
nest-box colonies, 20
 maintenance of, 26–7
 nest collection, 22–3
 pollen for, 27, 74–5
 queen collection, 25–6
nest-box designs, 24–5
nest odour, 23
nest-sites, 8, 10, 11, 13–14, 22
nesting
 carder bees, 10–11
 encouragement of, 24, 25
 orientation for nest location, 23
 short cycle species, 10, 20

oocytes, 72–3
ovaries, 16, 20, 72
 Psithyrus, 29
overwintering, 12–13
 honeybees, 12
 queens, 12–13, 19–20

parasites, 31–4
Parasitus fucorum, 32, 33
pheromones, 16
 and queen production, 16
pocket-makers, 7, 15, 16
pollen
 germinated, staining, 76
 identification, 44, 51; slide
  preparation, 75
 for nest-box colonies, 27, 74–5 •
 removal from bumblebees, 75–6
pollen baskets, 14, 42, 43, 53
pollen collection, 12, 14, 42–4
pollen-storers, 7, 15, 16
pollen tube staining, 76
pollination, 1
 bee introduction and crop
  yields, 3–4
 bee visiting patterns, 42
 best-adapted flowers, 49
 and hole-biting in corolla tube,
  8
 seed set evaluation, 50–1
predators, 34
Psithyrus (cuckoo bumblebees)
 flight levels, 19
 genital capsules, 48
 identification, 4, 54; females,
  67–8; males, 68–9
 male marking substances, 18
 natural history, 28–9
 ventral plate callosities, 47
Psithyrus barbutellus, 18, 47, 48,
 67, 69
Psithyrus bohemicus, 18, 19, 47, 48,
 68, 69, 82
Psithyrus campestris, 18, 19, 47, 48,
 67, 68
Psithyrus distinctus, 82
Psithyrus rupestris, 19, 47, 48, **67,
 68**
Psithyrus sylvestris, 18, 19, 47, 48,
 67, 68
Psithyrus vestalis, 47, 48, **68, 69**
pupation, 14

queens, 1, 6, 10, 11
 characteristics, 16
 collection, for nest-box
  colonies, 25–6
 dead, at nest sites, 14, 23
 emergence, and soil
  temperature, 6, 13
 overwintering, 12–13;
  appearance after, 19–20;
  behaviour after, 13–14
 parasites of, 32–4
 production, 15–16, 19
 seasonal flight activity, 9
 young, 17, 19, 20
 see also nesting

Scutacarus acarorum, 32, 33
sex determination, 16
sex identification, 55
spermatheca, 16
  sperm presence detection, 71, 72
Sphaerularia bombi, 32–4
sting sheaths, 45, 57
stings, 53, 55
  mating scars on base, 72
synonymy, 82

tongue lengths, 10
  determination, 73
  and foraging behaviour, 6, 8, 10–11, 41
Psithyrus, 29

ventral plate callosities, 47
Volucella bombylans, 30–1

water balance, 39
wax cells, 14
Wax Moth, 30
wing wear, 19–20, 73
wings, 54, 56
workers, 1, 6–8
  development, 14–15
  egg production by, 16–17
  seasonal flight activity, 9
  size of, and early feeding, 15

Maps (from ITE, 1980). Dots: records from 1960 onwards; open circles: a record before 1960 but not since.

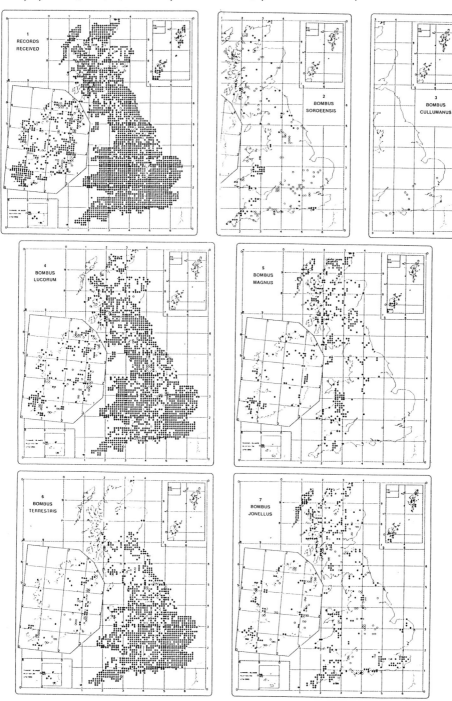

1 RECORDS RECEIVED

2 BOMBUS SOROEENSIS

3 BOMBUS CULLUMANUS

4 BOMBUS LUCORUM

5 BOMBUS MAGNUS

6 BOMBUS TERRESTRIS

7 BOMBUS JONELLUS

88

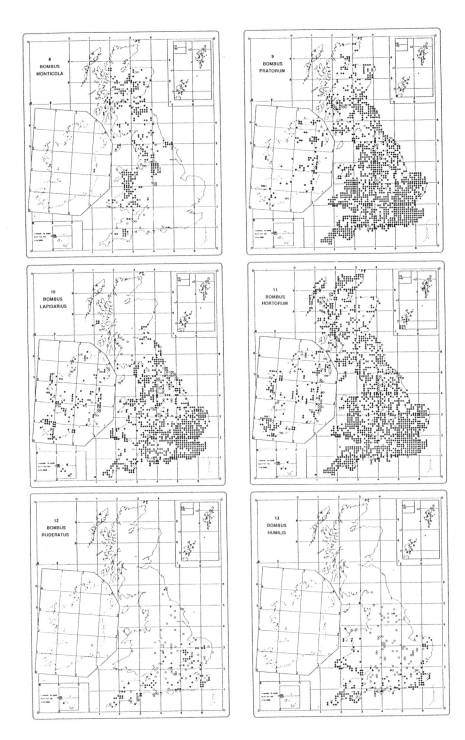

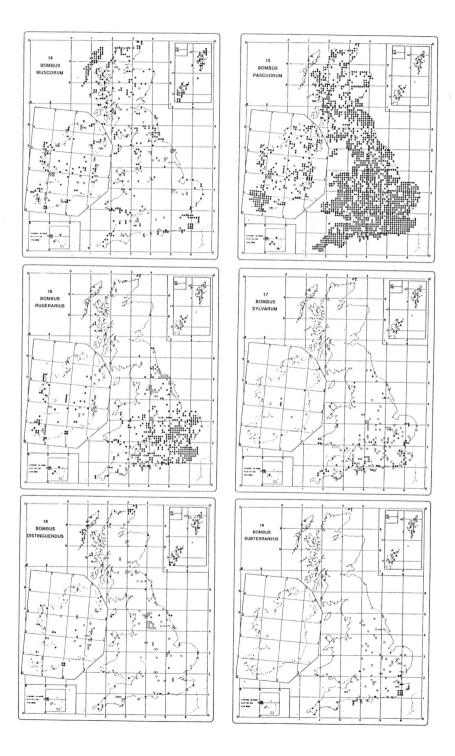

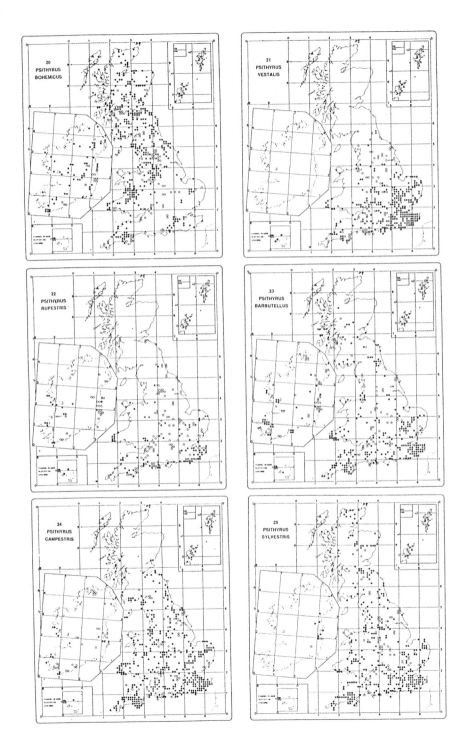

Addendum

Since the first edition of this book appeared, members of WATCH (junior wing of the Royal Society for Nature Conservation) and London Wildlife Trust have participated in a national survey to explore the flower preferences of the commoner British bumblebee species (Fussell and Corbet, in preparation). To reduce the risk of misidentification, bumblebees were identified to colour groups rather than to species, using a simple key similar to the Quick-Check Key on p. 55. The colour groups (and the commonest species in each) are: Browns (*B. pascuorum*); Black-bodied Red Tails (*B. lapidarius* and *B. ruderarius*); Banded Red Tails (*B. pratorum*, and also males of the Black-bodied Red Tail group); 2-banded White Tails (*B. terrestris* and *B. lucorum*); and 3-banded White Tails (*B. hortorum*). The key and the colour plates from this book are reproduced in a wallcard (Bumblebees wallcard (1987), available from The Richmond Publishing Co. Ltd., P.O. Box 963, Slough SL2 3RS) which participants received as part of the 'Really useful insects' project pack (WATCH, 1987; available from The Richmond Publishing Co. Ltd. or from WATCH, The Green, Witham Park, Lincoln LN5 7JR). Participants were asked to walk slowly along a selected route about 200–500 m long, noting the first flower visit of any bumblebee seen.

The survey showed that colour groups differed in the species of wild flowers, garden flowers and crops that they visited. Table 6 shows the species or species groups of plants visited by each colour group, listed in decreasing order of "simple selectivity", an index that takes into account the number of plant species available on each walk. Some of these plants achieve high scores simply because their flowers are numerous where they occur. Differences between bumblebee colour groups in flower choice are better represented by another index, "group-specific selectivity", that compares the proportion of one colour group's visits allocated to a given plant species on a walk with the proportion of visits allocated to that species by all other bee colour groups on the walk (Table 7). This index highlights dietary differences between bumblebee colour groups. The table includes plants that are not often recorded, but are much visited where they occur. It omits some which are known to be very attractive to bumblebees, but which were not recorded often enough for us to assess their score. One of these is *Phacelia tanacetifolia*, sometimes grown as a green manure crop.

Members of naturalists' groups are contributing to a continuing study of bumblebee nest sites, by supplying information about the habitat, aspect and position of any bumblebee nests they discover. In combination with the findings of the flower survey, the results are expected to help farmers to manage habitats to provide forage and nest sites suitable for bumblebee species important as pollinators of particular crops.

Table 6. *The top ten types of flowers visited by the five colour groups of bumblebees on at least 20 walks, ranked in descending order of 'simple selectivity', an index which takes into account the number of plant species available on each walk.*

2-banded White Tails	Black-bodied Red Tails	Banded Red Tails	Browns	3-banded White Tails
Rhododendron	Knapweeds	Knapweeds	Vetches	Rhododendron
Cotoneaster	Sedums	Snowberry	Himalayan Balsam	Foxglove
Buddleia	Campanulas	Cotoneaster	White Deadnettle	Delphinium/Larkspur
Bramble	Chives	Raspberry	Lavender	Red Clover
Willowherbs	Birdsfoot Trefoil	Ragwort	Woundworts	Woundworts
Lavender	White Clover	Lavender	Comfrey	Honeysuckle
Heather	Cotoneaster	Cranesbills	Catmint	Buddleia
Comfrey	Buttercups	Wild Thistles	Red Clover	White Deadnettle
Sedums	Rhododendron	Comfrey	Raspberry	Catmint
Knapweeds	Thistles	Rhododendron	Borage	Sage

Table 7. *The top ten types of flowers visited by each colour group of bumblebees on more than 5 walks, ranked in descending order of 'group-specific selectivity', an index which illustrates dietary differences between groups of bumblebees.*

2-banded White Tails	Black-bodied Red Tails	Banded Red Tails	Browns	3-banded White Tails
Hollyhock	Hawksbeards	Loganberry	Primrose	Delphinium/Larkspur
Hawthorn	Bluebell	Snowberry	Purple Loosestrife	Foxglove
Nasturtium	Gorse	Heuchera	Vetches	Pansy
Michaelmas Daisy	Birdsfoot Trefoil	Raspberry	Apple	Red Clover
Flowering Currant	Selfheal	Forget-me-nots	Wood Sage	Bindweeds
Azalea	Chives	Flowering Currant	Golden Rod	Teasel
Lupins	Aubrieta	Knapweeds	Meadow Vetchling	Toadflax
Columbine	Buttercups	Ragwort	Sallows	Honeysuckles
Himalayan Balsam	Hawkweeds	Cranesbills	White Deadnettle	Columbine
Golden Rod	Knapweeds (Garden)	Alkanet	Hyssop	Red Campion